The Sustainers

Being, Building and Doing Good through Activism in the Sacred Spaces of Civil Rights, Human Rights and Social Movements

Catherine Fleming Bruce

Selma to Montgomery National Historic Trail* Black Lives Matter Memorials* Medgar Evers House* Visanska Starks House and Carriage House* Freedom Riders Greyhound Bus Station* Audubon Ballroom* Lorraine Motel* Modjeska Monteith Simkins House* Robben Island Prison* Mother Emanuel AME Church*

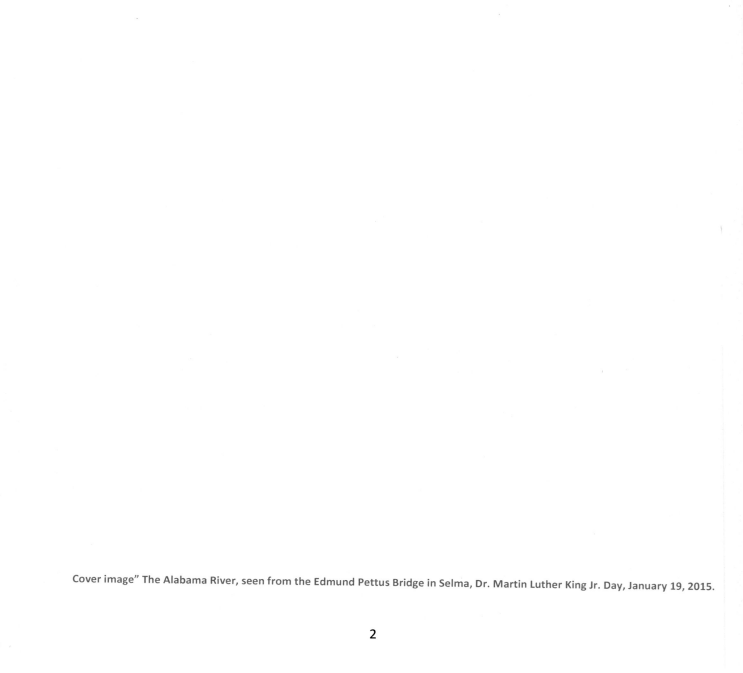

Cover image" The Alabama River, seen from the Edmund Pettus Bridge in Selma, Dr. Martin Luther King Jr. Day, January 19, 2015.

L to R: Selma to Montgomery National Historic Trail sign; Ezell Ford Jr. mural; Visanska Starks House; Freedom Riders Bus Museum; Stage in the Audubon Ballroom; Lorraine Motel; Medgar Evers House; Modjeska Simkins House; Robben Island.

Acknowledgements

My first thanks are to my family for their help and support through the years.

Special thanks for initial support from Janet Burnley, Melissa Abernathy, Betsy Shaw Brown, Charlotte Burch Jones, Carol Jones, Katherine M. 'Kit' Duffy, Cathy Armer, Crystal Washington and Dennis Adams.

I thank Anne Amma for the time she spent editing and strengthening my work, Justin Long for his formatting services, and Ginetta V. Hamilton and Kristen Sojourner for their example and encouragement. The glory is theirs; any oversight is mine.

For content insights, I thank Dr. Adia Benton, Frank Martin, my son Alaric Bruce, my brother Michel Fleming.

A heartfelt thanks to the Sustainers: Barbara Tagger, Minnie White Watson, Ray Arsenault, the late D'Army Bailey, Jerry Eisterhold, and to those who made the Sustainers event of 2013 possible: Dr. Vernon Burton, Kenneth Childs, Henry Fulmer and the South Caroliniana Society; the staff of the University of South Carolina's South Caroliniana Library; Ed Poliakoff and the late Stephen G. Morrison with Nelson, Mullins Riley and Scarborough Law Firm; Mayor Steven K. Benjamin and the City of Columbia; the South Carolina Association of Black Mayors, Richard Harpootlian and Bakari Middleton. Thanks to very special participants in and supporters of the Sustainers event: Rita Daniels and her family, descendants of Harriet Tubman with the support of Russell Simmons; Mayors Todd Strange, City of Montgomery, Alabama and A.C. Wharton, Jr. of Memphis, Tennessee.

Thanks to Ehren Foley, Ph.D., National Register of Historic Places, South Carolina Department of Archives and History; Herbert J. Hartsook, Director, South Carolina Political Collections, Thomas Cooper Library, University of South Carolina; the staff of the South Caroliniana Library, University of South Carolina; Sahm Venter and Lucia Raadschelders, the Nelson Mandela Foundation in South Africa; Reggie Hui, Jenna Smith, Library of Congress; Warner Brothers permissions Department; Mary Beth Sigado, Swarthmore College Peace Collection; Cindy Gardner, the Museum Division, Mississippi Department of Archives and History; the John F. Kennedy Presidential Library and Museum; the William Jefferson Clinton Presidential Library/NARA; my friends at Safe Federal Credit Union in West Columbia; George A. Brown; the staff of the New York Public Library and the Schomburg Center for Research in Black Culture, and the New York Landmarks Conservancy.

The Sustainers: (L-R) Judge D'Army Bailey, Barbara Tagger, Minnie White Watson, Jerry Eisterhold, (Harriet Tubman descendants Rita Daniels, and her mother, seated) Catherine Fleming Bruce, (opening presenter Vernon Burton) and Raymond Arsenault. October 2013.

Dedicated to my parents, Louis and Emma Fleming, Judge D'Army Bailey, and Katherine 'Kit' Duffy

A TNOVSA Publication

Printed in Charleston, South Carolina, United States of America

Publisher's Cataloging-in-Publication
(Provided by Quality Books, Inc.)

Bruce, Catherine Fleming, author.
   The sustainers : being, building and doing good
through activism in the sacred spaces of civil rights,
human rights and social movements / Catherine Fleming
Bruce. -- First edition.
   pages cm
   Includes bibliographical references and index.
   LCCN 2015914781
   ISBN 978-0-9962190-0-6

   1. African Americans--Civil rights--Pictorial works.
2. Civil rights movements--United States--History--
Pictorial works. 3. Historic sites--United States--
Pictorial works. 4. Social action--United States--
Pictorial works. 5. Human rights--United States--
Pictorial works. 6. Social movements--United States--
Pictorial works.   I. Title.

E185.61.B886 2015   323.1196'073
                   QBI15-600178

Manning Marable quote, pages xii, xiii: From *Living Black History: How Reimagining the African-American Past Can Remake America's Racial Future* by Manning Marable, copyright © 2006. Reprinted by permission of Basic Civitas Books, a member of The Perseus Books Group.

Contents

"There are places and moments in America where this nation's destiny has been decided. Many are sites of war -- Concord and Lexington, Appomattox, Gettysburg. Others are sites that symbolize the daring of America's character -- Independence Hall and Seneca Falls, Kitty Hawk and Cape Canaveral.

Selma is such a place. In one afternoon 50 years ago, so much of our turbulent history -- the stain of slavery and anguish of civil war; the yoke of segregation and tyranny of Jim Crow; the death of four little girls in Birmingham; and the dream of a Baptist preacher -- all that history met on this bridge."

Remarks by the President [Barack Obama] at the 50th Anniversary of the Selma to Montgomery Marches. Edmund Pettus Bridge, Selma, Alabama. March 7, 2015.

"The names of those who were incarcerated on Robben Island is a roll call of resistance fighters and democrats spanning over three centuries. If indeed this is a Cape of Good Hope, that hope owes much to the spirit of that legion of fighters and others of their caliber."

Nelson Mandela, Speech to the people of Cape Town after Parliament met to formally elect him President. Mandela would be inaugurated the following day in Pretoria. City Hall, Cape Town, South Africa, 9 May 1994.

"We come to Selma to be renewed. We come to Selma to be inspired. We come to Selma to be reminded that our work is not finished. Our country will never ever be the same because of what happened on this bridge."

Remarks by the Congressman John Lewis at the 50th Anniversary of the Selma to Montgomery Marches. Edmund Pettus Bridge, Selma, Alabama. March 7, 2015.

"Under the segregation laws, Black cab drivers cannot take white Freedom Riders to the hospital, and white drivers won't. Only the Catholic St. Jude's hospital will treat wounded Riders of any color. From his hospital bed, William Barbee tells reporters: "As soon as we've recovered from this, we'll start again." And from the white side of the segregated hospital, Zwerg agrees, saying: "We are prepared to die."

Bruce Hartford, We'll Never Turn Back, Civil Rights Movement Veterans website (crmvet.org).

"The Rev. Rhoda Montgomery was the preacher that day [January 15th], and while she apologized for the informality of her remarks she said something that will stick with me for a long time. She said that there is a marker in front of the Lorraine Motel in Memphis, the motel where Martin Luther King was shot, that is inscribed with words from the Book of Genesis. "You might expect something like an excerpt from his 'I have a dream' speech," she said. "You might expect the words that are on his tombstone: 'Free at last.' But what is written on that marker is a verse from the story of Joseph in Genesis, where his brothers say, 'Behold, here cometh the Dreamer. Let us slay him, and we shall see what will become of his dreams' (Genesis 37:19-20)."

Pastor Jim Somerville, "Here Cometh the Dreamer."

'Bill and Ellen Hirzy, of Washington, D.C., took time out from visiting family in St. Louis to pay their respects. Ellen Hirzy, 65, said, "I woke up this morning and said, 'I have to get over here.' I believe in making pilgrimages. At a place like this, you can absorb what happened."

Like many others who paused or prayed there, her husband was overcome with emotion. "To think about what happened here," Bill Hirzy, 78, a retired chemist, said as he dabbed at tears. "There's a spiritual feeling about this place."

Mull, who had watched police try to extinguish Tuesday's fire, said he and his neighbors want a permanent memorial at the scene. "Instead of a stain on the pavement, Michael Brown needs to be a mark on history," Mull said.'

Paul Hampel, *St. Louis Dispatch*, September 24, 2014.

"No break, all wake
Little mayhem for your All-State, nay ham, all steak
Get a good ball great like a golf grade
Make the ball break
Just one swing, no putting
That's how I try 'n does things, always
Especially when your past is
Martin, Baldwin, Audubon Ballroom"

Lupe Fiasco, 'Audubon Ballroom', Food and Liquor II: The Great American Rap Album, Part 1, 2012.

"Through his words, his deeds, his personal sacrifices and his many acts of courage, Medgar Evers is with us as we continue to press forward for final victory over wrongdoers whether they be in Mississippi, Alabama or Washington. On the day of triumph do not come to this softly-shaded grove to look for him, do not seek him in the tender earth of this bivouac of many who gave their lives at home and on foreign shores. Rather at that time when men sing the songs of triumph, listen for his voice."

Clarence Mitchell, NAACP Washington Bureau, Evers' Memorial Service June 13, 1965.

"The black leadership in South Carolina was in many ways in the vanguard of the civil rights movement in the South. As early as 1939, the black leadership [to include Dr. John Jacob Starks*] organized on a state level in an effort to combine forces and centralize the movement in order to increase their effectiveness. In 1944, Black South Carolinians instituted the first predominantly black state political party in the South during the twentieth century. In the late forties, massive registration campaigns added thousands of black South Carolinians to the public rolls. Additionally, the state's black leadership developed the Clarendon County lawsuit, the only case from the Deep South that was included in the renowned 1954 Brown vs. Board of Education of Topeka decision of the US Supreme Court. Modjeska Monteith Simkins was in the center of activities that were being planned and being carried out on a statewide level by Black South Carolinians during the *decades of the forties and fifties. By examining her public career, one gets a narrow but sharp perspective of the organizations and leaders of the movement for democracy and human rights in South Carolina."*

Barbara Woods, "Black Woman Activist in Twentieth Century South Carolina: Modjeska Monteith Simkins", 1978.

"Following a series of events and the singing of "America the Beautiful," Pinckney had given a homily. He read from the nineteenth chapter of Second Samuel, in which King David mourns the death of Absalom, the son who rebelled against him. Pinckney urged the audience to not only remember the ultimate sacrifice of so many but also to honor their sacrifice, by continuing to work toward the "great task" described by Lincoln in his Gettysburg Address. "Together we come to bury racism, to bury bigotry, and to resurrect and revive love, compassion, and tenderness."

Memorial in Charleston, June 19, 2015. Jack Bass/New Yorker, © Conde Nast.

*emphasis by the author

Introduction

Historical marker outside the Five & Dine Restaurant in Rock Hill, South Carolina, November 2014.

In January 2015, I joined other witnesses to the York County pardoning by Judge John C. Hayes III of the Friendship Nine, men who started the 'Jail No Bail' sit-in strategy through their activism in Rock Hill, South Carolina. Hayes' uncle, Billy Drennan Hayes, was the presiding judge over the 1961 case. The emotionally charged event drew such participants as retired South Carolina Supreme Court Chief Justice Ernest L. Finney and the Rev. Bernice King, daughter of the Rev. Dr. Martin Luther King, Jr., hundreds of spectators and droves of international media observers. We were all re-introduced and intimately touched by this story of people being good, building good, and doing good, at great personal sacrifice. The original building where the courage of those men was fully rendered is still in place, with a marker indicating its historic status.

Exterior of the former McCrory's Building, November 2014.

McCrory's Five and Dime stands where those men, as college students, broke an unjust law, were jailed and sentenced to hard labor on chain gangs in 1961. Owned at this writing by the Piedmont Regional Association of Realtors, the building underwent a 1.5 million dollar restoration, with original countertops and chairs refurbished and kept in place. The story of the Friendship nine is told through interpretive signage in the building's heritage hall, and through its historical marker. We see those men when we enter, and want to emulate their acts of goodness in some way.

Upon learning of the building's unique history, the new restaurant owners chose a name that would emphasize that history. Diners can occupy the barstools where the Friendship Nine sat, with the name of a protestor on the back of each chair. The presence of McCrory's as the new Five & Dine restaurant creates a tangible praxis, a combination of knowledge and action, in tandem with the very public court decision to expunge records of the Nine. It provides each visitor with an opportunity to recognize their works, though the action of saving a site that we recognize as sacred, and expanding and extending the good works of the Friendship Nine through this effort. The visitor can have one of the most intimate contacts that one can have with the Nine, one that helps them to know these men and their works, and to imitate them.

The original counter and barstools-each seat bears the name of a Friendship Nine member on the back, 2014.

York County Court rolls from 1961, shown January 28, 2015.

A member of the Friendship Nine shares an emotional moment with the Clerk as he finds his name on the 1961 roll, January 28, 2015.

Rev. Bernice King, daughter of Dr. Martin Luther King Jr., flanked by Friendship Nine member, the late Clarence Graham (her right) and York County Prosecutor Kevin Brackett (her left), speaks to the audience of the event's significance, January 28, 2015.

Presently, the Five & Dine operates this restaurant, and everyone recognizes the building as a unique space, which made protecting and restoring the building vital.

At the close of 2015, another set of nine chairs became synonymous with a story of racist hate, the will to fight against it, and the galvanizing power that a place could have: in this case, the basement of Mother Emanuel AME Church in Charleston, South Carolina, where nine parishioners were murdered in the summer of 2015. Anti-gun violence advocates laid a rose on each chair, and vowed to stand together to break the back of racism and the gun laws that weaponize racism's destructive force.

December 2015: Roses adorn nine chairs in the basement of Mother Emanuel AME Church, where black parishioners were slain by a white gunman.

Participants in an anti-gun violence campaign meet at Mother Emanuel AME Church in Charleston, December 2015.

This book is intended to be a place where readers encounter the stories of those who hallowed the grounds, those who sustained those grounds by ensuring their transformation and protection into landmarks, and others whose interactions with those grounds reach into us, calling us to re-enact good works in our own time. My personal journey as a sustainer of civil and human rights legacy sites made me curious to know about others who fought for the survival of locations where critical events in civil rights, human rights and social change movements had taken place. My path: the home of South Carolina civil rights activist Mary Modjeska Monteith Simkins and the Visanska Starks House and Carriage House in Columbia, South Carolina. To my mind, these and all fellow sustainers are heroes, because the road to salvation for these battlefields is long and hard, with many slick places and stones along the way. The years it takes to achieve the goal are accompanied with the knowledge that this portion of Movement history would by their efforts be well cemented in the public mind, and also with the lesson that those years of sacrifice would take their pound of flesh in some way. The names of some sustainers are never known or are beyond the scope of this writing, as the focus is on selected historical buildings rather than new constructions of civil rights museums and centers.

The builders, preservers, actors, scholars, storytellers and activists who are drawn to these sites hallow the grounds anew. We realize through these encounters that we ourselves can achieve as great a public good as those renowned for their labors and sacrifices in human struggles and movements. Transforming, restoring these sites to their proper places in public life, and sustaining existing public spaces has the effect of sustaining both the flame of many selfless acts, and the agility of those whose efforts to transform society and bring justice must continue to bear fruit. The stories in this book include the histories of those who have done good work and have left their mark, the stories of how places where the mark was laid were sustained, and how all are part of the same web of justice creation.

Part I – Being Good

This section tells the stories of landmark events at three sites, describing ways in which individuals personified good during their interactions with those historical spaces. It seeks answers from the standpoint of learning how these stories demonstrate human goodness, how they inspire goodness and action in us, and how these processes of learning and doing are sustained in the context of the sites over time. The places in this telling are **Visanska Starks House and Carriage House,** a lesser known site in Columbia SC; **Freedom Bus Riders – Greyhound Bus Station** in Montgomery where victory was snatched from the jaws of fear; and locations I call **#blacklivesmatter** sites, where the shooting deaths of unarmed African Americans by local law enforcement in 2014 were marked with memorials, launching a new chapter in social movements.

Part II – Building Good

This next book segment offers a view of some 'Sustainers' in activist mode; workers whose commitment insured that physical locations connected to the Movement were forever preserved. They "built good" by transforming their surroundings into challenging social and political institutions. The stories told in this segment offer proof that preserving the sites is an **extension** of the civil rights movement, is in itself a civil rights **action**. The places in this telling are the **Modjeska Simkins House** in Columbia SC; the **Audubon Ballroom** where Malcolm X was assassinated in New York City, and **Robben Island**, where South Africa's revolutionary, Nelson Mandela, was imprisoned.

Part III – Doing Good

Here in this segment, the good works of those who sacrificed are examined, along with how these works inform our lives, and how the sites capture and continue to reflect their energy. The focal points are the **Medgar Evers House** in Jackson, Mississippi where Evers died and woke the nation; the **Lorraine Motel** in Memphis where Rev. Dr. Martin Luther King, Jr. the dreamer was assassinated; and the **Selma to Montgomery March** National Historic Trail of triumph.

Part IV – Future Goods

This closing discussion, with the focus on the Mother Emanuel AME Church in Charleston, South Carolina, examines ways that this space, now venerated by a global audience, has advanced and expanded definitions of doing good. It also examines the limits and the frontiers of being good and doing good in these historical places. It asks if the money and energy invested in them have been better used in a more 'traditional' and direct social action? Would change under direct social action be a more authentic version of doing good? This section provides some answers to the challenges posed by activists and others. Finally, it explores ways that sites must:

- *Expand the strategies and goals of social and political movements;*
- *Move beyond discussion of rights, justice, equality and freedom concepts to political action and advocacy;*
- *Revitalize the public sphere, the arena in which extended occasions for thought and action can be developed;*
- *Provide space for generating unity through discourse, and space for deliberative, strategic and political ground work/grassroots organizing work.*

Group shot from the colloquium, 'The Sustainers', l to r: Rita Daniels, her sister and mother, descendants of Harriet Tubman; Dr. Vernon Burton, Kenneth Childs, and D'Army Bailey, at the Palmetto Club.

This book is the outgrowth of an event bringing some of these warriors together for the first time in Columbia, South Carolina for a colloquium entitled, 'The Sustainers: Builders and Preservers of Civil Rights Sites" held in October 2013. One inspiration for the colloquium was the 2012 announcement at the National Press Club in Washington that six Southern cities would hold the Civil Rights 50th Anniversary Commemoration the following year. The Mayors of Birmingham, Alabama; Columbia, South Carolina; Jackson, Mississippi; Memphis, Tennessee; Washington, DC; Selma, Alabama, Mayor George Patrick Evans; and Montgomery, Alabama, Mayor Todd Strange, would host commemorative events in their cities.

David Agnew, White House liaison to mayors, and Mayors Stephen K. Benjamin of Columbia, S.C.; William A. Bell of Birmingham, Ala., and Harvey Johnson, Jackson, Miss., announce the Civil Rights 50th Anniversary Commemoration, January 20, 2012. Scripps Howard Foundation wire photo by Jordain Carney.

As such, this work focuses primarily on the sustainers and sacred spaces which were part of those events geographically, along with a few additional sites. While the inclusion of all such sites is beyond the scope of this work, this is a place where the reader can share the stories of a few who ensured that hallowed grounds were transformed into landmarks, and can encounter those who retain the memories of heroic acts and personal sacrifices through moving image and re-enactments. For all of these actions constitute ongoing activism.

The purpose of the book is to share these stories with lovers of politics, culture, history and the arts, and with those who have a hunger to advance civil rights, human rights and other social justice movements. The hallowed grounds of our struggles draw actors, scholars, filmmakers, and activists who reshape the stories for new generations. This book welcomes the general and the specialized audience by including themes, topics and theories of global interest. While it is not a book targeted toward the academic and the scholarly audience, it welcomes their part of the story.

These publics, taken together, can generate the support and political will critical not only to saving civil rights sites, but also to ensure that the sites promote political engagement and social uplift of those most injured by discriminatory practices. The book presents the argument that civil rights, human rights and social movement sites, through <u>preservation</u>, through <u>creative inclusion</u> in film and television, through <u>re-enactments</u> and through specific types of <u>onsite activities,</u> CAN and MUST advance the achievement of a just and equitable present.

The Alabama River, seen from the Edmund Pettus Bridge in Selma, Dr. Martin Luther King Jr. Day, January 19, 2015.

Individual Activism and Sacred Spaces

Civil and human rights venerated spaces demonstrate that they are truly hallowed ground through a constant flow of stories and events that allow us to clearly see the common humanity in one another. These battlefields and consecrated spaces for justice are the examined and re-examined crossroads that bridge the gaps between ordinary people of different races, of men and women, religious groups and sexual orientations. The stories in this chapter focus on the leaders and legends connected with each site that gave their all for justice, but also includes those with whom we can readily identify: the volunteers, the students, the bystanders, and those who by speaking about their lives spark and energize movements. This chapter also enlarges the dialogue about preservation of these sites as advancement of civil and human rights movements, in combination with the activists and re-enactors who return year after year; and the storytellers who through varied venues recall and revalidate experiences directly from the fields of pain and glory.

Protesters in Ferguson, Missouri 2014.

#Blacklivesmatter Victim Memorials: Ferguson and Beyond

The stories of unarmed black persons, male and female, dying at the hands of law enforcement officers who are sworn to protect and defend, spreading like a wild fire through the tentacles of social media, have re-invigorated the desires of individuals to make change, not just in how persons are treated, but in how they are seen. Since the 2014 shooting death of Michael Brown, an unarmed black male, took place in Ferguson, Missouri, his body exposed on the ground for hours without medical attention and the decision of a grand jury not to indict the white police officer who killed him, this city, and many cities around the world have been the site of regular protests. But in some instances, the sites themselves have been made hallowed ground by the people of the community.

The sites explored here are connected to incidents of blacks killed by police, and do not share the same physical structure as the other historical locations. But they are no less sacred spaces. They have already exhibited to visitors their powerful connections to movements for civil and human rights in the United States and abroad. They teach the first lessons about the struggle for recognition that all individuals have intrinsic significance and goodness.

At the Canfield Drive location in Ferguson where Michael Brown was killed, a large memorial consisting of stuffed animals and other memorabilia had been in place since the August 2014 death. The site had been the subject of at least one desecration, when according to the *St. Louis Dispatch* newspaper, a car drove through it a few days before Christmas. Supporters immediately went to the social media venue Twitter to notify the public about the event, and by morning community members were there to reconstruct the memorial. Previously the memorial also caught fire, and had to be restored.

The erection of this site, and its subsequent protection, defense and formalization with a plaque installed on the first anniversary of Brown's death in 2015, reflect voices of those in the community who recognize the intrinsic good in the person of Michael Brown and are determined that others recognize this in him as well. Rather than seeing him written off as a statistic, or someone reduced to a particular set of social behaviors, the actions that were taken in creation of the memorial are an expression of his value in the eyes of his family and friends. One teddy bear, one flower, one picture at a time, an action without planning or strategy, but instead an impromptu weaving of a tapestry, reminding us that having Michael Brown in the world was good.

A march, along with the protests that followed, was sparked by the Grand Jury decision not to indict Darren Wilson, the white police officer who shot and killed Michael Brown. NAACP President and CEO Cornell Williams Brooks drew an immediate link between this march and the Selma to Montgomery March, held close to fifty years ago. Brooks spoke of the 'moral legacy' of that march, and connected the deaths of Michael Brown and Lowndes County Alabama resident Jimmy Lee Jackson, who also died at the hand of law enforcement, and whose death sparked the famous Alabama march. In making these connections, Brooks was doing more than joining the men by the manner of their deaths or by whom they were killed. He was also pointing to the good in these two young black men, in the face of far too many who do not see them in general as important and valuable, as citizens who contribute to their families and communities, as persons who had potential for greatness unrecognized by the mainstream.

The 'Journey for Justice' march started near the two Michael Brown memorials on Canfield Drive in Ferguson, Missouri, ending 120 miles later at the State Capital of Jefferson City, according to Huffington Post and Reuters news reports. The seven day march was a testament to the power of the Selma to Montgomery March, and the claim it has as a unifying and powerful force. The NAACP led the march, which began November 29, 2014 and ended December 6th. The starting point for the march, the memorial on the site where Michael Brown was killed, indicates that all protests would start with the memory of Brown, his place in the community, and the good that he represented to his neighbors.

The communal act of participating in the march that began at the memorial site allowed individuals to reflect the intrinsic good that Michael Brown carried, and amplify their voices in articulation of this good. America's Journey for Justice, an NAACP action commenced in 2015 from the

Edmund Pettus Bridge in Selma, would continue both the ties to the Ferguson, Missouri memorial site and the themes for social change that it represented.

Mural at the site of Ezell Ford Jr's death, August 2014.

On August 11, 2014, news reports surfaced of a memorial to Ezell Ford, a Los Angeles resident and unarmed African American victim of a police shooting. This memorial had stuffed animals and candles, but also a mural of Ford's likeness painted on the wall of a convenience store at the corner of 65th Street and Broadway in South Los Angeles, where the mentally ill man was killed. The mural may have been inspired by the Adrian Franks' image of another unarmed victim, Eric Garner, which was posted on film director Spike Lee's Facebook social media page and bore the quote "Our memorial for Eric Garner in front of our 40 Acres Headquarters in Da Republic of Brooklyn, New York". The New York space eventually expanded to include Mike Brown, Ezell Ford and John Crawford. But the site in California has the sacred effect, as 'ground zero' for the Ezell Ford murder.

While the identity of the visual artist who created Ford's mural is not broadly known, the work itself was noted in news coverage during the months after the murder. The mural served as a focal point and gathering place for family members and activists alike. The corner of 65th and Broadway was often the site for vigils, and for a moment for passerby to pause and reflect. Tritobia Ford, Ford's mother, and other family members and friends often participated in those memorials. The candles would be lit, and the mourners would remain to stand for Ford, to ensure that his memory would not be erased.

One principal virtue that reflects goodness is personal sacrifice. When the artist produced and contributed the mural without recognition or compensation, he or she shared the goods of his time and talent as an offering to communicate the value for Mr. Ford, who was sacrificed by those who did not see his value. Black Lives Matter groups have blossomed out to all parts of the country, and other organizations of empowered youth have grown strong in the heat of oppression. Their political experiences and engagements are rooted in their growing confidence, energy and hope, but they also feel the reinforcing power of these sacred spaces as they make standing up against change possible.

Visanska Starks House and Carriage House

Reflections on the lives of inhabitants of the Visanska Starks House and Carriage house in Columbia, South Carolina offers opportunities to examine multiple constructions of being good; in this case, through the inhabitants' willingness to foster emancipating institutions. The Reverend Dr. John Jacob Starks and Jewish community leader Barrett Visanska, both affiliated with the site in Columbia, SC, are examples of persons who influenced the development of civil and human rights through their

43

community actions. This section identifies the examples of their good works in enhancing education, developing institutions, promoting civil rights and advancing women's rights. This section also provides twenty-first century examples of social change connected to this site that contributed to the public good.

The discovery of the Visanska Starks Carriage House on this site, hidden under an old lean-to, gained national attention on Home and Garden Television (HGTV) series 'If Walls Could Talk" in 2007, airing internationally for several years afterward. But it was the dedication and willingness to move the property toward restoration, and to uncover its hidden racially and ethnically diverse history, its national and global connections, and its rich contribution to civil rights institution-building in South Carolina, that resulted in its expansion of public knowledge of those connected to the site who worked for good, and whose examples in strategy and work for justice that might be followed.

J. J. STARKS
Seneca Institute 1899-1912, Morris College 1912-1930, Benedict College 1930-

Setting the Stage for Student Organizing at Historically Black Colleges and Universities

Rev. Dr. John Jacob Starks lived in what is now the Visanska Starks House from 1938 until his death in 1944. Under Rev. Dr. Starks' leadership as its first black President in 1930, Benedict College served as a significant center of civil rights activities in South Carolina.

Stimulated by a national protest movement and the push in South Carolina from the State Negro Citizens Committee, led by Dr. Robert W. Nance and Mrs. [Modjeska Monteith] Andrew W. Simkins, Benedict College, Allen University and Claflin University students joined national youth demonstrations in protests against lynching on February 12, 1927. The formation of an NAACP branch on Benedict's campus, and the nationwide NAACP campaign for passage of the 1935 Costigan-Wagner Anti-Lynching Bill, was proof of campuses 'stirred to action' in 1937. Benedict College, with Starks as its first black President, and his encouragement of cooperation and shared space between Benedict and Allen University fostered this development. This was one of the first civil rights campaigns in South Carolina before World War II.

Levi G. Byrd. Undated.

Opening the Doors for Community Building

Levi G. Byrd, President of the NAACP in Cheraw, South Carolina, sought to energize his peers around the state and

45

across the South. He initiated an October 3rd 1939 letter writing campaign to urge formation of a statewide NAACP.

Byrd realized that support of Black Columbians was critical to power and success of a state organization. Through friendship and mentorship of Rev. Arthur Wright, father of Marian Wright Edelman, Byrd connected with the Dr. Starks, who offered Byrd an 'entrée to Columbia' through use of the College facility. By mid-October 1939, Byrd and Starks had agreed that the meeting would take place on Benedict's campus. Starks' movement to host the meeting at this institution provided the fledgling state conference with an 'air of legitimacy at a critical juncture in its history." The first statewide meeting of NAACP chapters was held in the library of Benedict College on November 10, 1939. Over twenty delegates from Cheraw, Charleston, Columbia, Florence, Georgetown, Greenville, Sumter attended and formally moved to formally initiate the State Conference of NAACP.

Good Works in the 1930's and 40's Changed the State and National Civil Rights Movement

Many think of the Civil Rights Movement as limited to actions that took place in the 1950's and 60's. The efforts of social actors like Rev. Dr. J.J. Starks underscore the significance of the 1930's and 40's in South Carolina, in particular, as a critical period for civil rights development leading to the strategies and actions of the Movement. Historian Erwin Hoffman, who documented the growth in South Carolina of the NAACP and the creation of Black civic organizations and institutions during those years, stated, "In the 1930's trends were established and personalities emerged that were to make much meaningful history in the field of equal rights in the years that followed. When interviewed in

1957, South Carolina Negro leaders remembered enough incidents of organization and struggle in prewar decades to support seeds of revolution were germinating and sometimes sprouting."

While a review of Civil Rights history research shows points of conflict regarding the dates of the Movement, the focus here is on the different categories of 'good works' that the Civil Rights agenda emphasized during these different time periods. According to Adam Fairclough, many historians agree that the Civil Rights movement dates were 1955-1968, known as the "Montgomery to Memphis" time-frame. The agenda of this period, led by Martin Luther King, Jr. and others as spokespersons, focused primarily on the elimination of racial violence and legalized, institutional segregation in education and in public accommodations. Fairclough further observes that in the wake of the 1944 *Smith v. Allwright* case, the beginning of the civil rights period was marked by increases in blacks becoming registered voters, as Medgar Evers and a fellow Alcorn A & M University student did in 1946, although their attempt to fulfill the right to vote was stopped by a mob of their white neighbors carrying baseball bats and guns. This event only sharpened Evers' determination to fight for his rights and the rights of others.

While Fairclough argues that some historians view the time after 1963 that some call the 'post-civil rights period', or 'the death of the civil rights movement', others like Clayborne Carson instead called it 'a black freedom struggle seeking a broader range of goals". Included in this expanded agenda are issues of poverty, access and equity, reparations, education, and media. Activists believed that these remedies would bring blacks excluded from public life into the fold, placing them on par with those who had previously been given more opportunity.

Writer Wim Roefs agrees that "the impact of 1930s and 40s activism in South Carolina with its early legalistic approach to civil rights, influenced the tactics of leaders from both sides in 1960s. Their actions set the stage for what would happen in the state and nation." Learning how these early progressives stayed involved in a struggle for rights over time informs present day organizing, and reminds activists that they need not wait for a 'movement' to engage in good works.

Uncovering the history of the Visanska Starks site provides further insights into how the NAACP in South Carolina was transformed from a small, urban-based organization focused on interests of a small class of black professionals, to a mass organization representing the needs of a broad cross section of black Carolinians across geographic, generational, and economic boundaries. Some concluded that the NAACP in South Carolina shaped the larger African American struggle for civil rights during peak years of its national influence. Historian Peter Lau argues: "By establishing a largely successful approach to reform that stayed within the law, 1930s and 40s movement leaders conditioned white politicians to accept moderate responses to civil rights reform, letting them know that moderate reform was possible." These tactics enabled 1960s civil rights movement leaders to balance younger and more strident activists' work with the more measured responses of elder reformers.

The early strength of the South Carolina Conference of NAACP allowed that organization to dominate the state's civil rights field. Through the 1940's to the 60's, the state's white establishment had to endure one of the strongest and fastest growing NAACP organizations in the country. Other adherents of the foundational role of 1930s and 40s activity on the South Carolina civil rights movement are historians Patricia Sullivan and John Egerton, who examined the South Carolina movement in both a regional and a national context. Barbara Woods' 1978 dissertation on Modjeska Simkins, an activist whose home site is also featured in this work, was also a forceful argument for the importance of these early struggles. A cadre of black leaders like Starks, who controlled institutions and organizations that paved the way for change in public life, by dissemination of information, by working to reform legislation, or by creating space and legitimacy for mass events, were critical to civil rights in South Carolina long before the 1960s. These leaders were the 'vanguard of the civil rights movement in the South'.

The Starks School of Theology and Students in the Struggle

Starks' Theological Seminary at Benedict College was the seedbed for numerous individuals who participated in the Civil Rights and social change movement in South Carolina. Dr. Starks was committed to spreading his work on theology; he completed theological studies at Morehouse College in Atlanta, Georgia, obtaining a Doctorate in Divinity in 1909. He was ordained to the full work of the ministry in 1898. His first pastorate was the Dunn Creek Baptist Church in Donalds, South Carolina, which he served two years. After that assignment, he pastored Ebenezer Baptist Church, at Seneca for six years; Canaan Baptist Church, at Cope, South Carolina for ten years, and Pleasant Hill Baptist Church, at Westminster, for four years. He served as a member of the Executive Board of the State Baptist Convention, and also was a pastor of Second Calvary Baptist Church in Columbia, South Carolina, a role he shared with NAACP leader Rev. James M. Hinton. Dr. Starks organized a School of Theology upon his arrival at Benedict College in 1930, with branches in at least one other South Carolina city; and many of its students were active in Civil Rights protests.

The April 1961 edition of *The Crisis* magazine noted that 'more than 100 students from Benedict College and Starks Theological Seminary are participating in the Columbia sit-ins which are "part of an all-out campaign that will persist until eating bias barriers are beaten", according to Rev. Isaiah DeQuincey Newman, NAACP field secretary in Columbia. Arrests were made at Eckerd's Pharmacy when store asked police to arrest demonstrators. Young people formed a picket line in front of the jail and police arrested 13 more for 'obstructing the sidewalk'. The South Carolina Conference of NAACP arranged bail. *The Crisis* further reported that 'NAACP sit-ins in Columbia are under the leadership of David Carter, age 26, president of the Benedict College Intercollegiate NAACP unit, and enrolled at Stark Theological Seminary at Benedict.'

Graduates and others affiliated with the Starks Theological Seminary include the following who worked with civil rights causes:

o **Rev. H.H. Singleton, II, activist, longtime President of the NAACP, Conway,** *South Carolina, received national attention for equal rights legal challenges he led.*

o **Rev. Roscoe C. Wilson, Sr., Pastor, St. John Baptist Church, Columbia,** *for 50 years; Wilson worked with civil rights leaders in their efforts to secure equal rights, treatment, and opportunities for residents in Crafts-Farrow Hospital, Bryan S. Dorn Veterans Administration Hospital and the SC Department of Corrections. He worked toward the integration of Baptist churches. The late Rev. Wilson, who passed in 2008, was the grandfather of A'ja Wilson, who propelled the University of South Carolina Lady Gamecocks basketball team to its first Final Four in history in 2015.*

- Dr. **Arthur William (A.W) Goforth, Zion Baptist Church pastor, Columbia;** *Williams held leadership positions in Operation PUSH, the NAACP, and was a member of the Human Relations Council of Columbia.*

- **Rev. Moses Javis, Jacksonville, Florida;** *a national Baptist church leader, was a Benedict college student participant in the NAACP Voter Registration Committee in South Carolina in 1960.*

- **Rev. Dr. S. C. Cureton, Greenville, President, National Baptist Convention, March-Sept. 1999** *(honored by 3372, a Resolution of the South Carolina General Assembly, 110th Session, 1993-1994.*

- **Rev. Dr. James William Sanders, Sr., Gaffney** *(honored by H. 3808, a Resolution of the South Carolina General Assembly, 118th Session, 2009-2010.*

- **Rev. Dr. Dorothy L. Pearson, Columbia** *(honored by H. 4261, a Resolution of the South Carolina General Assembly, 113th Session, 2009-2010.*

- **Rev. Sylvester Golden , Sr. Piedmont,** *(honored by H. 4388, a Resolution of the South Carolina General Assembly, 119th Session, 2011-2012.*

- **Rev. Willie Lee Buffington,** *founder, Faith Cabin Libraries, providing libraries when African Americans in* **South Carolina and Georgia** *had limited or no access. Buffington, a white Carolinian from Saluda, taught at Benedict College and helped build the Starks Theological Seminary library.*

- **Rev. Booker T. Sears, Jr. DD., Goodwill Baptist Church, Bronx, NY.**

- **Rev. Willie D. McMahand, Piedmont** *(honored by H. 4872, a Resolution of the South Carolina General Assembly, 114th Session, 2001-2002.*

The Rev. Dr. Starks and Educational Good Works

The Reverend Dr. John Jacob Starks spread good works across the state, through his lifelong leadership of Historically Black colleges and universities. Dr. Starks served as president of three historically black institutions during his lifetime: Seneca Institute (1899-1912), Morris College in Sumter (1912-1930) and Benedict College, as its first black president (1930-1944).

The Seneca Institute historical marker references Dr. Starks' service and its page on the online Historical Marker database provides Starks' biography. The Starks Center on the campus of Benedict College was named for Mrs. Julia Starks, wife of the President, and the Brawley-Starks Academic Success Center on the campus of Morris College is named for him. Though each of these institutions are vital to the education of African Americans, the National Register nomination form praised Benedict College, due to its emergence as one of the earliest Black colleges in the South, and the prominent role that it has and continues to play in black education in South Carolina and in the South.

Seneca Institute 1899 (top), Benedict College, 1930.

The Visanska-Starks Site and Good Samaritan: Black Nurses, and Women's History

The Visanska-Starks House is located next to Good Samaritan Waverly Hospital on Hampton Street in Waverly Historic District. Access to health care for blacks was a critical issue in the face of discriminatory practices by health workers during this period, and Dr. William Rhodes and his wife Lillian Rhodes responded by opening the Good Samaritan Hospital at 1508 Gregg Street in 1910. Benedict College also opened a hospital on its campus in 1920 to serve its students and employees. The Benedict Hospital merged with Waverly Hospital, which was founded by Dr. Norman A. Jenkins and his four brothers. At the time of the merger in 1926, Waverly Hospital was located in the former home of industrialist Lysander D. Childs on the corner of Hampton and Pine Streets, according to research by Sarah Frances Conlon. Waverly Hospital also held a nurses training school.

Good Samaritan and Waverly Hospitals merged into a single biracial board of trustees in 1938. The newly created Good Samaritan-Waverly Hospital was incorporated as a non-profit organization dedicated to providing health care and training for nurses. After the Good Samaritan and Waverly Hospitals merged in 1938 and the passing of Dr. J.J. Starks, the Visanska-Starks House became the Good Samaritan Waverly Hospital Nurses Home. It served in this capacity from 1946 until 1952, providing nearby lodging and peer support for the women who served as the hospital's nurses. However, a new facility was still desperately needed. Thanks to the efforts of Modjeska Simkins and other leaders, a new building opened as a licensed hospital and nurse training facility in September of 1952, serving as a much needed medical facility as well as Columbia's first purpose-built hospital for blacks. Once the new hospital opened, the Visanska-Starks House ended its purpose as the Nurse's home, but was the residence of a nurse, Mrs. Lula M. Cook and her family for several decades.

The Visanska Starks Site, Barrett Visanska, the Tree of Life Congregation, and Jewish Community Contributions to Civil Rights

Barrett Visanska, a Polish native who taught himself English on his trip to America by translating the King James version of the Bible, was a founder of Tree of Life Congregation in Columbia. A jeweler by trade, Visanska served as the Tree of Life's first Vice President and as President in 1902. He and his family purchased the Visanska-Starks House, and lived there from 1913 until the mid-1930's. In addition to proving the diverse nature of the community, strong leaders of this Jewish institution would contribute to the Civil Rights movement in Columbia and in South Carolina.

Rabbi Sidney Ballon was selected as Tree of Life's second rabbi in 1939, the Tree of Life's first resident rabbi since 1916. He served in that capacity until 1948, with absences due to World War II service. Ballon, a Rhode Island native and Phi Beta Kappa graduate of Brown University, was referred to as a 'strong leader' in Belinda and Richard Gergel's book on the Congregation. Ballon saw to it that the Tree of Life congregation participated in efforts to battle racial and religious discrimination in Columbia. In 1944, Rabbi Ballon attended a civil rights meeting of Atlanta's Southern Regional Council at Benedict College. Rev. James M. Hinton, head of Columbia NAACP and pastor of Second Calvary Baptist Church, was invited to speak at the Tree of Life Congregation in 1948. This fit the national context at the time, during which the Central Conference of American Rabbis (CCAR) issued a comprehensive statement "Judaism and Race Relations" in 1946, and served as an 'active voice for racial justice'.

Quieter, low-key support for civil rights was the tone over the next few decades, as many Jews in South Carolina, due to the widely reported warnings on their vulnerability in Southern society by Jewish public official Senator Solomon Blatt, bombings of synagogues in Atlanta, Charlotte,

Jacksonville, Miami and other Southern cities, and other reasons, were urged to caution. In contrast, on the national scene, seventy rabbis participated in the 1963 March on Washington with Dr. Martin Luther King, Jr. The Union of American Hebrew Congregations (UAHC) (now known as the Union for Reform Judaism [URJ]), invited Dr. King to be the keynote speaker at the 1963 UAHC convention.

In 1971, according to Gergel's research, the Tree of Life Congregation's Rabbi Michael Oppenheimer returned the institution to public efforts in the battle for racial and religious discrimination in Columbia, picking up a banner that had been carried by Rabbi Ballon. Working with a private, monthly luncheon group of black and white city leaders, Rabbi Oppenheimer participated in efforts that helped resolve racial tensions in Columbia in the early 1970s. He joined Jewish community leaders David Baker, and Senators Hyman S. Rubin and Isadore Lourie, in refusing to attend meetings at private clubs with discriminatory policies. In 1973, Oppenheimer was elected as the Columbia Ministers' Association's first non-Christian president, and his objections led the organization to conduct future meetings at sites under non-discriminatory policies. In this work Oppenheimer saw that the Tree of Life Congregation as an institution supported the ongoing work of Senator Rubin, whom he called "a stalwart activist and leader in the civil rights movement who was at the forefront of racial and religious integration in the 1960's". Rubin was a founder of the Columbia Community Relations Council and the Luncheon Club of Columbia, which was established solely for bi-racial social interaction and which has continued to thrive and is a model for similar groups around the State. Oppenheimer's efforts also supported the ongoing work of Senator Isadore Lourie, "a South Carolina State Senator from 1964 to 1992, who 'forced the state forward on civil rights when it preferred not to move', by authorizing legislation on public housing and affirmative action. US Senator Ernest Hollings noted that "Lourie came in with a passion to turn things around for African Americans, and poor white citizens, and nobody was going to stop him." Lourie's son Joel followed his father's footsteps and was elected to the South Carolina Senate. These individuals watered the good seeds of advocacy that fell from the Tree of Life planted by Mr. Visanska and others decades before.

Visanska Starks House and Carriage House: Modern Day Good Works

The Visanska Starks House is located in Waverly District, one of South Carolina's few African American residential districts listed in the National Register of Historic Places. After the Civil Rights Movement years had passed, the Visanska Starks site continued its role as a meeting place for civil and human rights efforts. One such group formed after the Emergency Conference on Racism, held October 24-26, 1996 in response to the church burnings that took place throughout the Southeast but primarily in South Carolina. Sponsors for the event included the National Council of Churches, the Center for Democratic Renewal, the Center for Constitutional Rights, and the South Carolina Local Organizing Committee.

President Bill Clinton's visit to Mt. Zion AME Church in Greeleyville, SC on June 12, 19 96.

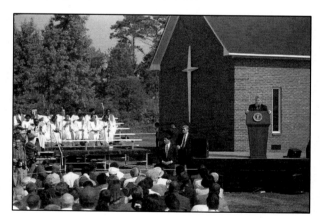

President Bill Clinton's visit to Mt. Zion AME Church in Greeleyville, SC on June 12, 1996.

The Conference followed President Bill Clinton's call for church burnings to become a national priority, and the establishment of a National Church Arson Task Force in June 1996, which combined the efforts of the Bureau of Alcohol Tobacco and Firearms, the Federal Bureau of Investigation, the Civil Rights Division, the Department of Justice, and other Federal, state and local agencies.

Women's International League for Peace and Freedom members Anne Braden (left) , Joan Watson, and Ruth Cadwallader (right) join Joan Watson at the Emergency Conference on Racism Columbia, SC October 24-26, 1996.

Rev. Dr. E. Gail Anderson Holness chaired the local organizing committee of the Emergency Conference on Racism. The engagement was broadened to include other Co-chairs: Burned Churches Coalition leader Reverend Terrance G. Mackey, Columbia NAACP leader Adell Adams, and Rev. Joseph Darby.   Author and activist Kevin Alexander Gray, a former organizer with Rev. Jesse Jackson's Presidential campaign, served as Rise Up March Against Racism Staff Coordinator; nationally known participants for the event included Dr. William Gibson, President of the SC Conference of NAACP;

journalist/activist Anne McCarty Braden and Rose Johnson, Center for Democratic Renewal; Ron Daniels, Center for Constitutional Rights; John Roy Harper, Columbia attorney and civil rights activist; David Bruck, death penalty activist; and Rev. Mac Charles Jones, National Council of Churches.

People protesting the burning of churches march on a Columbia, SC street heading for the State House and a rally of the National March of Solidarity to Challenge Hate in America, Saturday, April 12, 1997. Associated Press.

The South Carolina Burned Church Restoration Coalition had an office at 2200 Taylor Street, staffed by Rev. Cynthia Morris. This Coalition worked with the South Carolina Committee for Racial Justice and the Center for Democratic Renewal to host "A March of Solidarity to Challenge Hate in America" on April 11-12, 1997. Events on the 11th included a national press conference, a national public briefing on the status of Black Church burnings, a candlelight service and unveiling of the Black Church Burnings monument on Allen University's campus, and a Solidarity March and Rally starting at Allen University's campus and ending at the State House. In the aftermath of this effort, the South Carolina Committee for Racial Justice continued to meet at the Visanska Starks site. Members of this group included Rev. Leo Woodberry, Marion Fellowship of Churches; Corey Stevenson, South Carolina United Action; Kwadjo Campbell, the East Consortium; Kamau Marcharia, Grassroots leadership; James Sanderson, SC AFL-CIO; Kevin Alexander Gray; Rev Tom Summers, United Methodists; Brenda Reddix Smalls and Tom Turnipseed, Center for Democratic Renewal, among others.

Burned churches monument, Allen University grounds, Columbia, SC, 2014.

The Visanska Starks House was also connected to the Occupy movement through its owner's participation in the Occupy Columbia effort. The local offshoot of the Occupy Wall Street movement had chosen the South Carolina State House grounds as the site for their protest, and they remained there around the clock. On November 16, 2011, Governor Nikki Haley notified protesters that they had until 6:00 pm to leave the State House grounds. A rental truck was obtained to remove all of the Occupiers belongings, which included tents, blankets, tables and other equipment, until they could regroup and return to the State House. The truck delivered the items to the Visanska Starks House grounds, where they remained for a few days until they could be transferred to a secure storage space.

Gravesite of Rev. Dr. John Jacob Starks and his wife Julia, Palmetto Cemetery.

A group of the Occupiers who had been arrested filed a lawsuit, in which they accused the governor of failing to protect their rights to free speech and assembly. In 2014, the Governor and the State of South Carolina reached a settlement with those protestors, in the amount of $192,000.

Freedom Riders - Greyhound Bus Station

They were from Sumter and Columbia, Florence, Charleston and Great Falls, Charlotte and Durham, and Atlanta, Montgomery and Richmond, McComb and Jackson.

Throughout 1961, the Student Nonviolent Coordinating Committee (SNCC) challenged segregated transportation systems across state lines by sponsoring Freedom riders on buses in the South. A young John Lewis from Georgia, who would go on to represent his state in Congress, joined blacks and whites who boarded buses headed for Anniston and Montgomery, Alabama; Jackson, Mississippi and other cities.

They were from El Paso and Englewood, New Haven and Champaign, Shreveport and New Orleans, Newark and St. Paul, Saginaw and Detroit, Akron and Concord, Milwaukee and Oklahoma City.

The riders would include clergy, retirees, journalists, legislators, high school students, college faculty, elementary and high school teachers, union officials, artists, engineers, the unemployed and the underemployed, attorneys and researchers, housewives and social workers, executives and secretaries. The oldest was 61 and the youngest were 17, with the average being in their 20s and 30s.

They were from Boston and Baltimore, Houston and DC, Philadelphia and Providence, Spokane and Van Nuys.

The riders would include Bernard Lafayette, SNCC activist; Percy Sutton, attorney and New York NAACP Branch president; James L. Farmer, National Director, CORE; Jim Zwerg, a Beloit student and Fisk University exchange student; John R. Lewis, a student at American Baptist Theological Seminary; Bob Zellner, SNCC Field Secretary; C.T. Vivian, minister; Ralph Abernathy, Baptist Minister and SCLC leader; James L. Bevel, SNCC activist; James Forman, SNCC Executive Director; Tom Hayden, college journalist; and Fred Shuttlesworth, Alabama Christian Movement for Human Rights, SCLC co-founder.

They were from Buffalo and New York City, the Bronx and Rockaway, Brooklyn and Oceanside, Scarsdale and Long Island.

The riders would include students from Spelman College, Morehouse College, George Peabody College, Tennessee State University; Morris College, University of Cincinnati, Tulane University, Cornell University; Yale and Yale Divinity School, University of Minnesota, St. Louis University, City College in New York, Vanderbilt University; Howard University, Claflin University, Columbia University, Tougaloo

College, Virginia Union University, University of Wisconsin, University of California Berkeley, Texas Southern, University of California Los Angeles, Oakland City College, University of Toronto and University of British Columbia.

They were from LA and Berkeley, Tucson and Concord, Silver Springs and New Haven, Nashville and St. Louis, San Antonio and Chicago, Tampa and San Francisco, London and Munich.

Some would not participate again, and some would take multiple rides through dangerous and hostile cities and towns. The story of the freedom riders is one of the most powerful examples of individual courage and personal investment in making justice a reality; justice in the face of certain personal violence. The Freedom Riders were abandoned by those who were pledged to protect them, betrayed by local elected officials, and beaten with baseball bats, iron pipes and bicycle chains by fellow churchgoers who had just left religious services. Both President John F. Kennedy and Attorney General Robert Kennedy only reluctantly provided lifesaving protection. Inspired by the Journey for Reconciliation effort in the 1940's led by Bayard Rustin, these individuals, largely unknowns, involved in a most dangerous form of direct action brought America and its leaders face to face with its failures in democracy and in racial equality.

Federal marshals, wearing bright yellow armbands, keep an eye on the bus station after a band of freedom riders were beaten by a mob when they arrived from Birmingham the previous day, May 21, 1961. Associated Press.

Ray Arsenault.

Author Raymond Arsenault noted in his 2006 groundbreaking book "Freedom Riders", that 'the saga of the Freedom Rides deserves to be remembered in all of its meaning and nuance and, within the limits of human memory and the historian's craft, to be faithfully reconstructed for a society still grappling with the confounding issues of race, prejudice, and inequality". The former bus terminal in Montgomery, Alabama, the site and subject of violence, terror and bravery, became property of the US General Services Administration (GSA), listed on the National Register of Historic Places. With a lease agreement from GSA, the Alabama Historical Commission restored the building, to create the Freedom Rides Museum. The site also includes the courthouse where former US District Judge Frank M. Johnson Jr. presided over groundbreaking civil rights cases. After several fits and starts, the museum redesign by Ralph Applebaum Associates became a reality, and the site opened on May 1, 2011, commemorating the 50th anniversary of the Montgomery bus riots. The Museum opened along with other activities held from May 19-21, 2011 in Montgomery.

Arsenault is the John Hope Franklin Professor of Southern History at the University of South Florida, St. Petersburg, where he has taught since 1980. A specialist in the political, social, and environmental history of the American South, he has also taught at the University of Minnesota, Brandeis University, the University of Chicago, and the Universite d'Angers, in France, where he was a Fulbright Lecturer in 1984-85. Arsenault is the author or editor of seven books, including *Crucible of*

Liberty: 200 Years of the Bill of Rights (1991); and *Freedom Riders: 1961* and the *Struggle for Racial Justice* (2006). *Freedom Riders* was named an Editor's Choice by the New York Times Book Review, a Best Books of 2006 selection by the Washington Post Bookworld; and an Honorable Mention Best Book of 2006 by the Gustavus Myers Center for the Study of Bigotry and Human Rights. The abridged edition of Freedom Riders, published in 2013, is the companion volume to the PBS Emmy Award winning American Experience documentary film, *Freedom Riders* (2011), directed by MacArthur Fellow Stanley Nelson, who apprenticed with William Greaves, and also produced *The Black Press: Soldiers Without Swords* (1999), *The Murder of Emmett Till* (2003), *Wounded Knee* (2009), *Freedom Summer* (2014) and *Black Panthers: Vanguard of the Revolution* (2015).

The year 2013 marked the release of the PBS documentary 'Freedom Riders', by veteran filmmaker Stanley Nelson, based on the book by Raymond Arsenault. Congressman John Lewis, a Freedom Rider at the time who sustained serious injuries, remains in the forefront of the civil rights effort, chairing the Congressional Faith and Politics Institute, which has led pilgrimages to civil rights sites in Alabama since 1998. Interviews with Nelson, Arsenault, Congressman Lewis, and other surviving Freedom Riders focus on the role that the Freedom Bus Riders - Greyhound station continues to play in supporting past hopes and future leadership. Arsenault's book, years in the making, and Nelson's PBS documentary on the subject of the freedom riders are also credible examples of individual efforts to sustain and transform the legacy of civil rights workers whose faces and words would have otherwise been unknown and invisible to the popular consciousness. The phenomenon of youth boldly taking risks in the face of change continues unabated today, and gives fresh hope for a turning of the world toward a truer representation of justice.

The Audubon Ballroom stage, shortly after Malcolm X was assassinated, February 21, 1965.

Advancing the Common Good by Guarding Hallowed Grounds

Audubon Ballroom

The Audubon Ballroom in Harlem, New York was named for 19th century artist John Jay Audubon, one of the world's foremost students of birds and their habitats. Audubon, who lived in the Harlem neighborhood of Manhattan, was the son of a creole woman of color and a French sea captain. Scholar Manning Marable noted in his book on the life of Malcolm X that the "carvings of exotic birds on the foyer", were inspired by the ornithologist. It would be the Audubon that attracted Malcolm X upon his return to Harlem as the location from which to speak to the community about freedom and justice. It was the place where he would be assassinated.

Malcolm X journeyed from his life in Nebraska where his father was murdered by the Ku Klux Klan and where he and his siblings were separated, to his transformative imprisonment to leadership in the Nation of Islam (NOI). His speaking engagements while in the service of the NOI brought him to many places, including Clark University in Worcester, Massachusetts on April 29, 1963 at the invitation of D'Army Bailey, a Worcester Student Movement leader who would one day restore the Lorraine Motel where Dr. Martin Luther King Jr. was assassinated.

Malcolm's break with the NOI in March of 1964 led him free to formulate new ideology and direction. According to historian William Sales, the focus of that direction would be the development of an organization aligning the African American Civil Rights struggle with the international human rights movement. He wanted to spark a 'transition from reform to revolution', a revolution inspired by and connected to the people of Africa, who emerged from colonialism to take over the helm of their own nation states. Malcolm's travels to the Middle East, his pilgrimage to Mecca and his visit to several African nations were designed to develop partnerships and strategies to strengthen this new organization.

Malcolm X addressing a rally held by the Organization of Afro-American Unity (OAAU) at the Audubon Ballroom, in New York City, as Zanzibari Pan-Africanist Abdul Rahman Mohamed Babu (Seated at far right), listens. December 1964.

Malcolm concluded his global explorations, returned to Harlem, and on June 28, 1964, launched the Organization of Afro-American Unity (OAAU) with a press statement delivered from the stage of the Audubon Ballroom. In his speech, Malcolm talked about the importance of Harlem as one of the cities with the highest populations of African Americans. He outlined a plan to "bring about the complete independence of people of African descent here in the Western Hemisphere, and first here in the United States, and bring about the freedom of these people by any means necessary". The plan, with cultural, educational, and political components, was closely modeled after that of the Organization of African Unity, formed in 1963.

Starting from that day in June, each Sunday the OAAU would hold a rally from the stage of the Audubon Ballroom, to build Malcolm's movement. On July 5th, he focused on the need for the African American struggle for civil rights to be seen as a world struggle, without which, the world would have no peace. He urged Black organizations to work cooperatively toward this end. On November 29th, he shared his experience at a summit of African leaders in Cairo, and the pride it gave him to be in "a beautiful place" where Heads of State who looked like him discussed political and economic matters from a revolutionary perspective. On December 20th he urged his audience to look at America, and their lives in America, from a global perspective, reminding them that they were not struggling alone. Looking across the oceans to what was happening in African nations, and reaching out to work together would forge the vision of Pan-Africanism that Malcolm felt was critical to the American transition struggle.

On January 24, 1965, Malcolm X began the New Year with a focus on the importance of history and self-knowledge in the struggle for Black independence. He described African Americans without this knowledge as 'stumps' and 'trees without roots' who were easily destroyed, while those who learned their past history of greatness would be motivated to repeat that greatness. The following month, the last of his life, Malcolm would travel to Selma, Alabama, to deliver a speech for the Student Nonviolent Coordinating Council, known as SNCC. This February 4th speech was an outgrowth of OAAU's commitment to forming alliances with youth activist groups like SNCC. The speech was held at Brown Chapel AME Church, one of the landmark buildings of the Selma to Montgomery National Trail. This commitment resonated with activists such as Congressman John Lewis years later, as an event shared with Selma visitors over the years.

Later in the month, only a day after Malcolm's house was firebombed, he returned to the Audubon to talk with his community about worldwide revolution. He spoke of his recent meetings with President Julius Nyerere of Tanzania; with Jomo Kenyatta who had become President of the newly formed Republic of Kenya a few months before; with Ugandan Prime Minister Milton Obote, President Kwame Nkrumah of Ghana, President Sekou Toure of Guinea, and President Nnamdi Azikiew of

The Malcolm X and Betty Shabazz Center entrance.

Nigeria. Malcolm described outreach efforts to unite the African American, the Cuban, Caribbean and the African communities, and then to unite those communities with Asian communities as groundbreaking, and necessary for true global liberation. "The understanding that I got," Malcolm noted, 'broadened my scope so much that I felt I could see the problems and complaints of Black people in America and the Western Hemisphere with much greater clarity."

Malcolm X maximized every moment in the Audubon to the service of his goals in the revolution. His final Sunday at the Audubon, February 21, 1965, would be the day of his assassination.

Building Good Together: A New York City Collective

It would take four decades for the site of Malcolm's assassination to achieve its transformation. As film director Spike Lee wrapped up production of *Malcolm X*, Columbia University was mired in controversy about plans to demolish the Audubon Ballroom. After a period of vacancy and deterioration for the building, the City of New York acquired the property. Columbia University, Mayor David Dinkins and the City of New York reached an agreement in 1983, with the goal of gaining space to create a biomedical research park in partnership with the City and State of New York. Kemba Johnson, Associate Editor of local watchdog publication *City Limits*, noted that efforts to landmark the Audubon were rebuffed at this time, as the New York City Landmarks Preservation Commission refused to hold a hearing on the matter.

Although University leaders and Mayor Dinkins were convinced that demolition of the Audubon was a good that would bring jobs and development to Harlem, the process immediately became contentious. Main movers in saving the site of Malcolm X's assassination from demolition were Betty Shabazz, Ruth Messinger, Edward Kaufman and Franny Eberhart, along with vocal protests from Columbia University students and community leaders Gilbert D. Moore, Omawali Clay, and Michael Henry Adams.

Gilbert D. Moore.

Gilbert D. Moore at the Brooklyn Museum.

Gilbert D. Moore, represented the Sugar Hill Historical Society at public hearings on the issue. His work as a historic preservationist and community organizer was preceded by employment as a reporter for *Time* magazine, assistant editor of Time-Life Books, contributor to *Life*, *Newsweek*, *New York magazine*, *Ms. Magazine*, *Essence* and *Change*, as well as editing the Community News Service in Harlem and teaching at Rutgers University and Livingston College. In a later interview for a publication of the Brooklyn Museum, Moore described the 'uproar' that the request for demolition caused, because of the building's historical and architectural significance. Moore formed the Sugar Hill, a Harlem-based historical society, to support his interest in preserving the Audubon and spaces similar to it.

Also speaking in favor of saving the building was Omowale Clay, representing the Malcolm X Save the Audubon Coalition, an *adhoc* group formed in February 1990 to preserve the building and the legacy of Malcolm X. Clay had been arrested, tried and acquitted as a member of the New York 8 and the December 12 movement.

Omowale Clay.

Michael Henry Adams.

C. Virginia Fields, an activist and Birmingham, Alabama native, served as member of New York City Council, representing the district which includes Harlem. She was active in the effort to save the Audubon along with Michael Henry Adams, a local preservationist, historian and author. Adams continued to work closely with the Harlem area, staging a one man protest over demolition plans for the Renaissance Ballroom, which led to his arrest.

On April 13, 1990, 150 members of Columbia's Coalition to Save the Audubon, composed of students, faculty and members of the December 12 movement protested Columbia University's plans. On December 14, 1992, hundreds of Columbia University students blocked Hamilton Hall, held demonstrations and formed picket lines to protest the demolition of the Audubon Ballroom. Reverend Calvin Butts, minister of Harlem's Abyssinian Baptist Church, assisted with hours of negotiations with students. Three students were suspended over the incident and scores of others disciplined. The vocal

Ruth Messinger.

Franny Eberhart.

opposition of these individuals and organizations generated significant public pressure, and the site of Malcolm X assassination was eventually saved by a compromise which allowed some demolition to move forward to make way for the new building, while preserving key portions of the original Audubon Ballroom. Betty Shabazz, the widow of Malcolm X, was critical to this compromise, as she expressed her desire that the building be preserved and that Malcolm's legacy be memorialized in connection with the building in which his life ended.

On top of this support, the permission of the Manhattan Borough was needed in order for the project to receive federal funding, and it was Manhattan Borough president Ruth Messinger who was able to use this leverage to argue for preservation of the Audubon Ballroom. Her dedication helped to insure that portions of the original Audubon would survive the contentious process, which included Columbia University students occupying Hamilton Building on its campus in protest. Local observers credited Ms. Messinger and others for contributing to a plan approved by the New York City Board of Estimate, which mandated that Columbia University, rather than demolish the Audubon Ballroom, agree to keep and preserve its façade on Broadway, its lobby, and a portion of the Ballroom, including the stage, the site of the assassination.

Franny Eberhart, representing the New York City Landmarks Conservancy, and Edward Kaufman, a spokesman for the Municipal Art Society, also presented in favor of saving the building. Kaufman's role was also critical to the preservation of the building where Malcolm X was assassinated; it was he who assembled architects who created a blueprint design for a new building around original components. However, other actions included in the agreement that would provide additional funding support for the Aububon Ballroom stalled with the transfer of power, and change to a new Mayoral administration.

Manning Marable.

Scholar Manning Marable described his engagement in and support of the restoration project as City and University plans were announced in 1983, and pushed back to 1990 in the wake of negative response. Marable became more immediately involved when the new building opened in 1995, but a rent subsidy from Chase Manhattan Bank arranged by Mayor Dinkins to support the Audubon did not survive the transition to Mayor Rudolph Giuliani. Dr. Betty Shabazz died on June 23, 1997, a victim of injuries caused by a tragic fire started by her young grandson Malcolm, who himself would die tragically in 2013. With no further progress on the Audubon site, Marable agreed to assist Malcolm's third oldest daughter, Ilyasah Shabazz, in completing the Audubon project. The grand opening of the Malcolm X and Dr. Betty Shabazz Memorial and Education Center finally took place on May 19, 2005.

The sequences in Spike Lee's film, itself the result of years of work with producer Marvin Worth and screenwriter Arnold Perl, sequences which depict Malcolm's assassination in the Audubon, constitute the last opportunity for the ballroom to be filmed before portions of the building were demolished to make way for a new Columbia University structure.

)enzel Washington plays the lead in the assassination scene of the 1992 Warner Brothers motion picture *Malcolm X.*

Academy Award winning actor Denzel Washington, who had played Malcolm on stage, stood on the Audubon stage to portray the revolutionary's last moments, and would later receive an Oscar nomination for his performance. The film and the ballroom stood in testimony to the tragedy of loss that must be overcome, and the warrior's work that must continue.

Malaak, (left) and Ilyasah, (right) Daughters of Malcolm X and Betty Shabazz at the opening of the Center.

Some visitors to the Center express remorse that so much of its original structure and fabric had been destroyed, with only a shell of the original façade and stage remaining. But one of the daughters of Malcolm X and Betty Shabazz, Ilyasah Shabazz, who authored a book on her life growing up as a daughter of the famous activist, expressed her ongoing commitment to the role that the Ballroom would continue to play as an extension of Malcolm X's political priorities and as a physical and cultural icon.

There is equal social good in the Audubon as a physical and cultural icon and as a political force. Poet and activist Sonia Sanchez continuously emphasized the value of culture in the Movement. Alex Haley extended the theme of cultural consciousness, in his famous *Autobiography of Malcolm X*, recalling how Malcolm X once burst out of the driver's side door of a car they were riding in together past the Schomberg Center, to chastise a group of youth who he felt were showing disrespect to a building committed to protecting the cultural heritage and identity of Black Americans.

Likewise, the Audubon Ballroom, and the good works that Malcolm X attempted to construct through his work with the OAUU, are both continuously reconstructed through various users and uses, all with a potential for the power and voice that might emerge in the future.

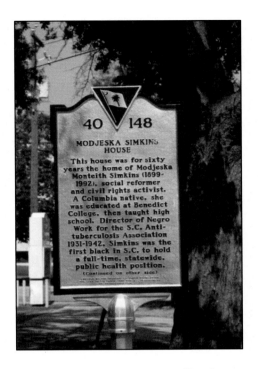 

Modjeska Monteith Simkins House

In November 1949, Modjeska Simkins sat in the living room of her Marion Street home in Columbia, South Carolina with Reverend Joseph A. DeLaine. Together they drafted the petition that would be signed by the more than 100 black parents in Clarendon County, South Carolina suing for equality of education for their children. The suit, *Briggs vs. Elliott,* would become the second case in *Brown vs. Board of Education*, argued before the United States Supreme Court by NAACP lawyer Thurgood Marshall.

The Modjeska Simkins House, as one of the National Register's relatively small number of historic places dedicated to a woman, is most unique in its connection to the *Briggs. V. Elliott* and

Brown v. Board of Education cases. A 1991 television movie featuring the cases, *'Separate But Equal'* directed by George Stevens, Jr. and starring Sidney Poitier and Burt Lancaster, was filmed partially in Columbia, South Carolina. Historian Charles Joyner wrote: "The importance of Modjeska Simkins in the history of the South Carolina NAACP – [and as a result, to the NAACP national cases] and in the pursuit of equal justice in South Carolina – would be difficult to overstate". Mary Modjeska Monteith Simkins, a Columbia native and contemporary of Coretta Scott King, Rosa Parks and Septima Clark, was known as "the Matriarch of the South Carolina civil rights movement."

Modjeska with independent film director Joan Harvey, 1982.

As chair of the program committee and member of the executive board of the Columbia NAACP, Simkins helped found the statewide organization, becoming the only female founder and officer of the South Carolina Conference of NAACP in 1939. She served as secretary of the group from

1941 to 1957, helping win teacher salary equalization lawsuits in the cities of Sumter and Columbia, writing news articles for the Associated Negro Press, and educating African Americans about voting while covering a statewide speaking circuit.

Simkins House 1995.

Throughout her career in social reform, Simkins used her private residence as her primary office from which she launched regular letters to the editor, her campaign to establish the Good Samaritan Waverly Hospital to serve the needs of Black citizens, as well as a meeting place and lodging for fellow workers who were often denied rooms in segregated Columbia hotels. Some of these 'fellow workers' included Robert Carter of the NAACP Legal Defense Fund, Andrew Young and Jesse Jackson.

The national NAACP's first legal defense fund team in Washington, headed by Charles Hamilton Houston, Bill Hastie, Thurgood Marshall, and assisted by Jack Greenberg, initiated cases in several southern states as part of their national legal campaign for public justice. Thurgood Marshall, Robert Carter and Jack Greenberg came to South Carolina to try these cases as early as 1938. Thus, these South Carolina cases have national significance, as part of the National Strategy by the NAACP Legal Defense Fund. Marshall would go on in 1967 to become the first black Supreme Court Justice.

Mrs. Simkins was close to the out-of-court preparations in South Carolina and exerted influence in a personal way. Several of the NAACP attorneys carrying out the major civil rights cases in South Carolina stayed in Modjeska and Andrew Simkins' home. In particular, Thurgood Marshall was a frequent guest. Most of the counsel's strategic planning sessions were held in the dining room. Interviews with Mrs. Simkins revealing this were included in the 1989 PBS documentary 'Road to Brown'.

In 1996, Simkins' reflections were also recorded in a series of interviews for the Public Radio International special 'Will the Circle Be Unbroken: A Personal History of the Civil Rights Movement in Five Southern Communities", produced by George King for the Southern Regional Council. Other interviewees were NAACP leader and Pastor James M. Hinton, Federal Judge Matthew J. Perry, Jr., historian Jack Bass, and editor of the *Lighthouse and Informer* John McCray. The interviewees and other participants of the radio program were honored in a kickoff event at the University of South Carolina, with the assistance of Dr. Grace Jordan McFadden.

Historians, legislators and the general public acknowledge the national significance of the *Briggs v. Elliot* case, with regard to the *Brown et. Al. v. Board of Education of Topeka* decision. Legal experts argue that the case is nationally significant because of Judge J. Waties Waring's dissent, the language of which made up Thurgood Marshall's argument before the Supreme Court. The case was also significant because it was the first of the individual cases to reach the Supreme Court, prior to its being folded into the other cases of Brown.

Elizabeth Cady Stanton, nineteenth century women's rights activist, noted that "history is silent concerning the part women performed". She tried to address that challenge by contributing to the preservation of historic sites that interpret the lives of American women. A review by historian Vivien Ellen Rose in 1997 noted that of the 1,942 properties listed as National Historic Landmarks in 1990, less than two percent preserve women's past. Rose also noted that there are only about sixty historic sites that are open to visitors seeking information about women's efforts to shape American life. In addition, identifying women's leadership in building national movements can also be overlooked. Barbara Tagger, in surveying landmarks in the Southeast, noted that few acknowledged female leadership of the modern civil rights movement. This was the context in which the Simkins House Restoration took place.

Self portrait of the author.

Building Good: Sustaining the Legacy of Activist Modjeska Simkins through Site Restoration

In 1990, the author spoke with a staff member of the South Carolina Arts Commission, who was acquainted with Mrs. Mary Modjeska Monteith Simkins. He remarked, 'someone ought to do a documentary on her life'. Knowing little about the civil rights activist at the time, but struck by the man's reverence for this woman, the author explored the idea. Finding that an SCETV documentary about Simkins' life was in progress, the focus shifted to a history of Blacks in Columbia. Entitled, *A Perfect Equality: Conflicts and Achievements of Historic Black Columbia*, the video documentary was completed in 1993. It was through this early conversation that the seeds were sown for the author's encounter with Mrs. Simkins and saving the historic house.

Dr. Barbara Woods.

A reading of Dr. Barbara Woods' 1978 dissertation on Simkins' life: "Black woman activist in twentieth century South Carolina: Modjeska Monteith Simkins", presented the broad sphere of influence that she was connected to, and all that she had accomplished and stood for. During the process of conducting several interviews with Mrs. Simkins for *A Perfect Equality,* the author proposed that the house should one day be a center for human rights. With one hand on her mason jar of water, Simkins waved the other, saying "I'm not worrying about that. That's for future generations to think about". Despite her humility, others had begun to officially recognize her; in 1991, the City of Columbia under the leadership of Mayor Bob Coble named December 5th "Modjeska

Monteith Simkins Day," prompted by the South Carolina Women's Consortium's desire to honor her 92nd birthday. It was to be her last.

When Modjeska Monteith Simkins passed away on April 5, 1992, the author sat on her porch, where she used to feed the birds, instead of attending the large funeral, confident that the preservation of this sacred space, where so much public good had been built, was already in motion. That confidence lasted until a preservation selection committee of which she was a member reviewed submissions to South Carolina's most endangered historic sites list, and found the Simkins house among the entrees. It turned out that the family members had made inquiries, but no avenue appeared to bear fruit. Some family members were concerned that other family members were willing to sell the property for commercial purposes, which would in no way preserve her legacy.

Martha Monteith, left, and Henrie Monteith Treadwell with a framed portrait of Modjeska Monteith Simkins that they donated to the University of South Carolina's South Caroliniana Library.

Also in 1992, shortly after Simkins' death, University of South Carolina Public History graduate student Jill K. Hanson approached Simkins' sister in law, Mrs. Martha Monteith and her niece, Dr. Henrie Monteith Treadwell, with the offer to develop and submit the application to designate the house as a historic landmark. With their approval, Hanson prepared the application, which included a full history of the house supported by deeds, City and County records and other documents, detailed description of its interior and exterior architectural style, photographs and maps. The significance of Simkins' life, her contributions to social change and events that took place in her house came mainly from the work of primary scholarly work of Dr. Barbara Woods and University of North Carolina Chapel Hill Oral Historian Dr. Jacquelyn Hall, supported by local and state newspaper articles.

Hanson submitted the application in October 1993. The State Historic Preservation Office approved the application on February 18, 1994 and on March 25, 1994 the Modjeska Simkins House was officially entered into the National Register of Historic Places. Although this was a major step forward for the site, that in itself offered no respite. In the meantime, the City of Columbia had marked the house for demolition, since it had been vacant since Simkins' death in 1992 and was in poor condition. A demolition notice was posted in 1995.

Simkins House interior, pre-restoration.

Simkins House rear porch, pre-restoration.

Simkins House exterior, pre-restoration.

Simkins House interior, pre-restoration.

After conversations with the estate co-executrix, Henri Monteith Treadwell, her attorney Kenneth B. Wingate, and preservationist Ray Sigmon, the author gathered a group of people to roll up collective sleeves and work on saving this sacred space. Further service included assisting the executrix in erecting a tombstone for Simkins' gravesite at Palmetto Cemetery, and submitting its inscription for approval. A presentation was made to Probate Court so that the Simkins House could be separated from her estate and the restoration project launched. That accomplished, the funds were raised for the purchase and the stabilization, and slowly, the renovation of the Simkins House. Kenneth Wingate, who provided valuable legal insights for the project in its early stages, went on to become interim State Treasurer during the Governor Mark Sanford administration, and Chair of the Commission on Higher Education during the Sanford and Haley administrations, would later receive the Order of the Palmetto, sharing the state's highest honor, with Modjeska Simkins and others. Dr. Monteith Treadwell also had a civil rights legacy of her own, as one of the three pioneering black students who integrated the University of South Carolina in 1963.

Cassandra Williams Rush, Environmental Health Science.

Michael G. Geronimakis, Geronimos Environmental Consultants.

One of the initial requirements of the South Carolina Department of Archives and History grant was an environmental site assessment. This assessment with conducted by Michael G. Geronimakis, P.E. , currently of Geronimos Environmental Consultants, and Cassandra Williams Rush, the African American proprietor of Environmental Health Science in Columbia. The assessment consisted of interviews, site visits, historical review, and an environmental records review.

The Modjeska Monteith Simkins House Restoration Project, initiated in 1995, received the generous support of such institutions as Carolina First Bank, the South Carolina Department of Parks,

Recreation and Tourism, the W.K. Kellogg Foundation, the City of Columbia, South Carolina Department of Archives and History, Richland County, UNUM Colonial Life, the Monteith Holding Company, the Hootie and the Blowfish Foundation, the National Trust for Historic Preservation, Fund for Southern Communities, Benedict College, Bank of America, the Sisters of Charity Foundation, the South Carolina American Civil Liberties Union, and City Year.

Church volunteers pose for a group picture before beginning a day of service at the Simkins House.

Churches, schools and community organizations offered their willing hands to support the Simkins House renovation, and to volunteer their time. City Year volunteers and University of South Carolina students participated in the annual King Day of Service each year for several years. Business and corporations also generously donated time and labor to the cause. The Wisteria Garden Club, an African American organization, provided volunteer planting time.

95

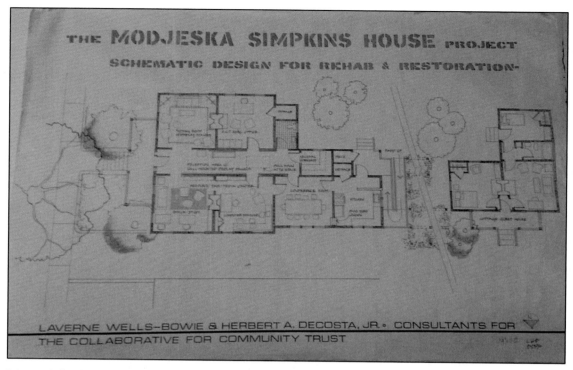

Schematic for the restoration, submitted by Herbert A. Decosta Jr. and Laverne Wells-Bowie.

The Modjeska Simkins House restoration was one of those rare projects that almost everyone was excited about, and wanted to participate in. Those business owners who desired additional parking space and hoped to see the building bulldozed were not among them, but on the whole, the community benefitted greatly from the restoration of this sacred space. Other community members stepped up in a big way to help. Contributors included the University of South Carolina Women in Law program, with Race Judicata funds raised to support renovation. A play was performed by University of South Carolina theatre department, under the direction of Thorne Compton, to raise funds for the Simkins House restoration project. University of South Carolina public history graduate students, under then chair Robert Weyeneth, came to help with removing the old torn and worn wallpaper. Colonial Life employees also came and helped clear the overgrown brush in the backyard. Some of them even suffered cuts and scrapes in the process.

The preservation of the house led to the recovery of other documents that highlighted Modjeska's life. Mrs. Simkins had been awarded the Order of the Palmetto during the administration of Governor Carroll A. Campbell, Jr., who served the State from 1987 to 1995. The document could not be located, and a replacement was requested. However, instead of receiving a duplicate, the award was bestowed by the new governor, David M. Beasley. Modjeska Simkins may be the only South Carolinian in history to receive two Order of the Palmetto awards from two different Governors.

With direction from renowned architects Herbert A. DeCosta Jr., and LaVerne Wells-Bowie and the hands and tools of contractor Johnny Martin with Martin Construction, the house was opened as a Civil and Human Rights Center in 2005. Photographs of *Briggs v. Elliott* plaintiffs, taken by Clarendon County native Mary Louise Miller, were displayed there, along with a copy of the Briggs petition from the South Carolina Department of Archives and History. Collection and preservation of the items and documents found in the two buildings and on the Simkins grounds were a top priority. The University of South Carolina's Public History department played a great role in this by arranging for graduate students to assist in these tasks. Matthew Hebert, Georgette Mayo and J. R. Fennell expertly identified documented and stored artifacts and ephemera for future exhibit purposes. All three went on to practice their craft in major institutions in and out of South Carolina.

Herbert A. DeCosta Jr.

Laverne Wells-Bowie.

Matthew Hebert.

J.R. Fennell.

The ten year effort concluded with the property becoming a permanent addition to Columbia's historic landscape in 2007, with its transfer to the City of Columbia and the Historic Columbia Foundation establishing annual base funding, including a major grant from Save America's Treasures, a federal preservation initiative started by First Lady Hillary Clinton. Barbara Tagger, well known for her work with National Park Service sites, underscored the significance of such restoration projects, noting the sparse number of historic sites, structures and landscapes that interpret the history of African American women. In 1997 her research found that only two National Park Service affiliated sites 'commemorated African American women's contributions to US history. Visitors learned about Modjeska Simkins and her many contributions to South Carolina and the nation, including:

- o *The end of discriminatory public transportation practices in the state and region, desegregation of the University of South Carolina.*
- o *Desegregation of public schools across the nation, through Briggs v. Elliott and Brown v. Board of Education, and the work of Thurgood Marshall.*
- o *Voting rights and access to health care for all South Carolinians.*

At that time, of the 800 sites listed in the African American National Register of Historic Places sites, only 50 dealt with contributions of women. The publication featured only three women, Mary Church Terrill, Mary McLeod Bethune, and Elizabeth Harden Gilmore.

Simkins House, (left); National Register plaque, acquired through the SC Department of Archives and History in 2005 (above).

After the launch of the Modjeska Simkins House Restoration project, the academic and popular scholarship on Simkins' life of good works increased dramatically. Before 1995, most of the scholarly work on Simkins was done by Barbara Abacha Woods, in articles drawn from her dissertation, a few South Carolina historians, and oral history work conducted by Jacqueline Hall at the University of North Carolina Chapel Hill. Between 2005, the year the historic house opened and 2014, there were over 50 scholarly works with reference to Simkins' life, including a dissertation on her leadership on the Good Samaritan Waverly Hospital project for African Americans during segregation, as well as other books and dissertations ranging from mass communication to politics to religion. The Modjeska Simkins Papers are held in South Carolina Political Collections, housed in the Ernest F. Hollings Library at the

University of South Carolina's Thomas Cooper Library. Interviews conducted with Mrs. Simkins are now part of the William A. Elwood Civil Rights Lawyer Documentary Project manuscript collection at the University of Virginia. The restoration of Simkins' house helped to move her from a marginalized figure to one now firmly established and highly visible in local, regional and national civil rights history, and inclusion in the poetic work of National Book Award winner Nikky Finney.

The Simkins House restoration also provided a way for South Carolina to have greater popular inclusion in the physical civil rights narrative of the nation. Placing the House in the digital record was critical, and so was added to the National Park Service website "We Shall Overcome: Historic Places In the Civil Rights Movement" in 2005. Members of the 50th Anniversary of *Brown vs. Board of Education* Commission visited the site during observances held in South Carolina.

Community event held at the Simkins House during its restoration.

Another was the inclusion of the House as a stop during the anniversary of Freedom Summer, led by Ben Chaney, brother of James Earl Chaney, murdered along with fellow civil rights workers

Andrew Goodman and Michael Schwerner in Philadelphia, Mississippi on June 21, 1964. While Civil Rights tourism flourished in other cities, Columbia was regularly bypassed. The development of the Simkins House led to Columbia's inclusion in Freedom Summer Ride for Justice Anniversary tours in 1999 and in 2004.

A briefcase under the cottage at the Modjeska Simkins Center was left by the Columbia City bomb team investigating a possible threat to the building Thursday, December 14, 2006, in Columbia, SC. Associated Press.

Freedom Summer 1999 was a project of the Chaney, Goodman, Schwerner Unity Coalition, and was supported by the Religious Action Center of Reform Judaism and the NAACP, in honor of the 35th Anniversary of the Mississippi Freedom Summer project, organized in 1964 by the Council of Federated Organizations (COFO), a coalition of the Southern Christian Leadership Conference (SCLC), the Student Nonviolent Coordinating Committee (SNCC), the National Association for the Advancement of Colored People (NAACP), and the Congress on Racial Equality (CORE).

President Lyndon B. Johnson meets with Civil Rights leaders Martin Luther King, Jr., SCLC; Whitney Young, National Urban League, and James Farmer, CORE. January 18 1964. Source: Lyndon Baines Johnson Library and Museum.

These efforts, along with the murders of Goodman, Chaney and Schwerner are cited by many as leading to the Civil Rights Act, passed by Congress in 1964, which provided an end to legalized racial discrimination in education, transportation, accommodations and the employment markets.

The 1999 Freedom Summer tour began in New York City, and came through Washington DC, Greensboro, North Carolina; Columbia, SC; Atlanta GA; Birmingham and Selma, Alabama and ended in Philadelphia, Mississippi. Prior to the Modjeska Monteith Simkins House restoration, such civil rights tours would not have included Columbia. The house gave them a reason to come through. Freedom Summer 2004 marked the 40th Anniversary of the events, reported in this journal entry from one of the participants:

> *"Today, we were very warmly welcomed by the Columbia, South Carolina, community. The People's Agenda of South Carolina provided us with a delicious Southern meal....a good thing since food in the previous days was few and far between. After a moving ceremony honoring the slain Freedom Riders Chaney, Goodman, and Schwerner, the freedom riders took a tour of the home of Modjeska Simkins, a South Carolina civil rights activist. We then proceeded to a neighborhood of Columbia in which we divided up into teams and fanned out to register voters. The Freedom Riders registered 75 new voters and met many already registered voters who had kind words of encouragement."*

The Simkins House was a gathering place for locals on the death of Rosa Parks in October 2005. It was also a stop for Presidential candidates in 2004. Sen. Joseph Lieberman made it the first stop on his Poverty tour. Gen. Wesley Clark used the site as a place to meet with South Carolina black press. Clark was accompanied by US representative Charles Rangel.

Left: General Wesley Clark, 2004 presidential candidate and US Congressman Charles Rangel visit with the South Carolina black press, Right: Richard Samuel Rodgers photograph of Modjeska Simkins.

The portrait on the wall behind the two men embodies a special element of building good. The portrait is a rare photograph of Modjeska as a young woman, taken by African American photographer and Columbia resident Richard Samuel Roberts, a Florida native who relocated to South Carolina in 1920, and was active in his photography studio throughout the 1920's and 1930's. According to press released by Algonquin Books of Chapel Hill, North Carolina and Bruccoli Clark of Columbia, three thousand glass photographic plates were stored in the crawlspace under Samuels' house at 1717 Wayne Street in Columbia, after Roberts passed away and his photography studio was closed. In 1977, Dr. Thomas L. Johnson, the Field Archivist and Assistant Director of the University of South Carolina's South Caroliniana Library was conducting interviews with Roberts' son Cornelius, who at the time was living in the Wayne Street family home. Johnson learned from him of the existence of the plates, which the family had kept for almost fifty years because they were convinced of their historical, social and artistic value.

Johnson had the idea to publish a book on Roberts and his work, and Matthew J. Bruccoli, President of Bruccoli Clark Publications of Columbia, agreed. In a 1983 letter to the Roberts family, Bruccoli noted 'it is clear to us that [Roberts] was a highly gifted photographer whose work has enduring significance. We are honored by the opportunity to publish his work". With permission and special arrangement with the Roberts family, the 179 boxes of glass plate negatives, found to be in excellent condition, and were delicately removed from under the house by the family, then carefully cleaned, restored and printed by Dr. Phillip C. Dunn, a University of South Carolina member of the Art Department faculty and photography expert. Johnson conducted an oral history of Roberts, and worked with Dunn to bring the photographs to Columbia's black community for identification. Johnson and Dunn, in collaboration with photographer's children, Mrs. Wilhelmina Roberts Wynn, Mr. Beverly N. Roberts, Mr. Cornelius C. Roberts and Mr. Gerald E. Roberts, chose 189 of the best photographs to present in a book: "A True Likeness: The Black South of Richard Samuel Roberts", published in the Fall of 1986.

Of the 4,000 images on the almost 3,000 glass plates, one fortunately included was the youthful photograph of Modjeska. Flipping through the pages of 'A True Likeness', the author happened upon it, and sent a request to Matthew Bruccoli, owner of Bruccoli Clark. He graciously gave his permission for the photograph to be reproduced for display in the Modjeska Simkins House. The portrait was printed directly from the glass plate negative that was hidden under the house, with the assistance of Thomas

Johnson. The image resulting from this process was a rare exhibition quality print. This print was entrusted to Columbia artist Rodgers Boykin for framing. Boykin returned with a joke that the portrait was damaged in the process before presenting the beautifully framed work that still hangs in the Simkins House.

Long before the formation of the effort to preserve Mrs. Simkins' House, this rare glass plate negative of Modjeska sat in cool repose under the Arsenal Hill house, waiting to be made public. Johnson noted in his article in the *State Magazine* that the family use of this hiding place away from the Columbia summer heat, was a 'stroke of good fortune that historians, archivists and preservationists dream about – and celebrate'. The restored and published works, too have been celebrated, particularly for those who learn about Modjeska Simkins to view her as a young woman, presented gracefully and artfully by the self-taught artist who moved to his wife's hometown, created and built the equipment for his photography studio on 1119 Washington St, and provided images that Philip Dunn felt surpassed even the master of Harlem Renaissance photography, James Van Der Zee.

Rodgers Boykin, Columbia artist, framer for works in Modjeska Simkins House.

When the City of Columbia joined other Southern cities in observances of civil rights events in 2013, and the Columbia63 effort was initiated, Mrs. Simkins's contributions to that history and the historic place itself were well situated to be an important component of the physical and social history of Columbia that would be the ongoing work of historical institutions, activists and individuals scholars. The good that Modjeska build can be felt with each visit to her home, and the energy that formed her work continues to build good.

Burial site for Modjeska Monteith Simkins and her family members, Palmetto Cemetery, Columbia SC.

Cell block in Robben Island Prison, South Africa.

Robben Island Prison

On October 9, 1963, Nelson Mandela stood in a Rivonia courtroom facing a formal charge of sabotage against the government of South Africa. Mandela was already a prisoner when the trial started, as he was arrested on August 5, 1962 and stood trial for leaving the country without a passport and inciting workers to strike. He was convicted and sentenced to five years in prison on November 7, 1962. The Rivonia sabotage trial would end on June 12, 1964.

American activists Malcolm X, John Lewis, Harry Belafonte and Diane Nash had all traveled to Africa in that year, part of the burgeoning and purposeful connectedness being created between members of the African Diaspora. Mandela had been writing and speaking out against the government's policies of apartheid, a system separating persons by racial and ethnic groups, and denying them civil and human rights. He was convicted on June 11, and the next day sentenced to life imprisonment. On June 13, Mandela was remanded to Robben island prison, where he would be held for 18 years.

On March 31, 1982 he was transferred to Pollmoor Prison on the mainland. This period was marked with health struggles, with Mandela admitted on August 12, 1988 to one hospital and then another, being treated for tuberculosis over a four month period. On December 7th of that year Mandela was transferred to Victor Verster Prison in the western cape of South Africa, and released from there on February 11, 1990, having been imprisoned for 27 and a half years. His confinement, the death of activist Steve Biko, and the unceasing resistance of Black South Afrikan people was picked up in one country and then another, until the voices calling for an end to apartheid were echoing around the world. South Africa became a pariah country, its athletes barred from international competition, its products blocked by boycotts from the global market, its institutions shrinking from disinvestment. Nelson Mandela's freedom, the result of international political and economic pressure, and the development of the seldom seen leader as a global human rights icon, was formalized by South African President F.W. de Klerk.

AFRICAN CHRISTIAN DEMOCRATIC PARTY		ACDP
AFRICAN DEMOCRATIC MOVEMENT		ADM
AFRICAN MODERATES CONGRESS PARTY		AMCP
AFRICAN NATIONAL CONGRESS		ANC
DEMOCRATIC PARTY - DEMOKRATIESE PARTY		DP
DIKWANKWETLA PARTY OF SOUTH AFRICA		DPSA
FEDERAL PARTY		FP
LUSO - SOUTH AFRICAN PARTY		LUSAP

Section of South Africa's first national ballot in 1994.

The nation's first election in which all races and ethnicities could participate would take place four years later, an election that would lead to Mandela's historic presidency.

Justin Chadwick's 2013 film 'Long Walk to Freedom: Nelson Mandela Story' was the result of three years of research, and included a meticulous replica of Robben island prison on a set in Cape Town. In the authentic telling and retelling of civil rights stories, acknowledgement of the fields of pain and glory are critical. The physical locations are the touchstone for everyone who encounters them. In many cases, old prison facilities are demolished. But this one provided an opportunity for Nelson Mandela to build additional good.

Ahmed Kathrada, right, with Nelson Mandela.

Andre Odendaal.

Nelson Mandela, Ahmed Kathrada, Andre Odendaal

In 1991, a change came over Robben Island prison, and its final political prisoners passed through the doors. Nelson Mandela visited the empty prison in 1993, according to his recollection in 'Long Walk to Freedom'. It stood empty until 1996, when it formally closed, and was named a National Monument. In 1997, then President Nelson Mandela reopened the former prison as the Robben Island Museum. In 1999 it gained World Heritage status with UNESCO.

The founding CEO of the Robben Island Museum was Professor Andre Odendaal. The effort to establish a museum was a collective decision which included Nelson Mandela, Mr. Mandela's co-accused in the Rivonia Trial and a former Robben Island prisoner, Ahmed Kathrada. Kathrada, who later spoke at Mr. Mandela's state funeral on December 15, 2013, became the founding chairperson of the Robben Island Museum Council and remained so until 2005. Mr. Sibongiseni Mkhize joined Robben Island Museum in 2010 as its CEO.

Robben Island is described as a 'contentious space which celebrates the triumph of the human spirit over trials, tribulation, and social and political injustices.' At the official opening of the new Museum in 1997, Mandela had these words:

> *"How do we reflect the fact that the people of South Africa as a whole, together with the international community, turned one of the world's most notorious symbols of racist oppression into a worldwide icon of the universality of human rights, of hope, peace and reconciliation? I am confident that we will together find a way to combine the many dimensions of the island and that we will do so in a manner that recognizes above all its preeminent character as a symbol of the victory of the human spirit over political oppression; and for reconciliation over enforced division."*

Thus, for many, the idea of Robben Island as a sacred space is rooted in Mandela's lifetime of experience and sacrifice to build good. Martti Ahtisaari, President of Finland from 1994 to 2000, reflected this view in his remarks upon receiving the 2000 J. William Fulbright Prize for International Understanding, whose first recipient was Nelson Mandela:

> *"In my office, I have two paintings and a piece of quarry rock from Robben Island given to me by President Mandela. The maximum security prison on Robben Island is where Mandela spent the bulk of his 27 year imprisonment. The piece of rock symbolizes for me the persistence and determination that can overcome even the greatest difficulties. If reminds my visitors and me daily that no problem is too difficult to be solved. This lesson of persistence is one that I would like to carry across to my own continent."*

Ahtisaari spoke of the need for these virtues in building good through structures that would aid in resolving international conflict. These efforts include his work with the United Nation's Transition Assistance Group in Namibia from 1989 to 1990, and his work in the 1990s as chairman of the Bosnia-Herzegovinia Working Group of the International Conference on the Former Yugoslavia, and the United Nations secretary-general's special representative to the former Yugoslavia.   While the continuing conflict in the Middle East, the emergence of ISIS, the terrorist attacks in France, Turkey, Belgium, Nigeria and elsewhere, and the growing refugee crisis provide ongoing challenges throughout the globe, historic hallowed spaces can affirm the work of those who continue to work for peace and justice, and an end to strife and inequality around the world.

Enriching the Civil Rights Information Landscape

Lorraine Motel

Room 306 at the Lorraine Motel in Memphis, Tennessee, was known as 'The King-Abernathy Suite' due to the frequency of SCLC leaders Dr. Martin Luther King Jr., and Rev. Ralph Abernathy there, according to Abernathy's testimony to the House Select Committee on Assassinations on August 14, 1978. Almost a decade earlier, on the evening of April 4, 1968, Dr. King was standing on the balcony of this motel room. As he turned to go in, a shot was fired, entering his right cheek, breaking his jaw and neck, shattering several vertebrae and severing his jugular vein. Abernathy and Andrew Young rushed to his aid, pointing out the direction from which the gunfire came, and saw that King was transported to St. Joseph's Hospital, where he was pronounced dead.

US House Select Committee on Assassinations representatives Yvonne Braithwaite Burke, California(upper left); Walter Fauntroy, District of Columbia(second from upper left); and Chair Louis Stokes, Ohio (fifth from upper left) listen to witness testimony on the assassinations of Dr. Martin Luther King, Jr. and President John F. Kennedy.

At this writing, the Honorable Andrew Young Jr. and the Rev. Jesse Jackson Jr. are the last surviving individuals who were with Dr. King at the time and location of his murder, at the Lorraine Motel. The Filmways Productions 1978 television miniseries *King*, featuring Paul Winfield and Cicely Tyson, depicted the assassination without using the Lorraine Motel. The purchase of the property in the 1980s generated copious media interest. It was the opening salvo in the battle to save this sacred space and transform it into the International Civil Rights Museum in Memphis.

Flyer advertising the sale of the Lorraine Motel after King's assassination.

Foreclosure Auction flyer for the Lorraine Motel.

D'Army Bailey , Benjamin Lawless and Gerald Eisterhold

After the King assassination, although owner Walter Lane Bailey preserved rooms 306 and 308, the motel was decaying and threatened with extinction and foreclosure. The quiet time that it spent in its decay was a result of the disquieting effect it had on almost everyone who encountered it. D'Army Bailey was a notable exception, reflecting:

Dec. 13, 1982, Judge Bailey holding the winning bid card at moment of purchase of Lorraine Motel on courthouse steps foreclosure auction.

"For 23 years, it was almost as if the mere sight of the Motel and the memories seeing it evoked were too painful to acknowledge, as if looking at it would dredge up all the hate and anger and heartbreak that had been focused here back in April 1968. Instead of preserving the Lorraine, the City had allowed it – like the South Main Street neighborhood surrounding it – to deteriorate into a collection of neglected brownstones and moldering warehouses. I felt that the time for collective denial was over, and that the opening of the National Civil Rights Museum signified a positive step toward helping the City live the dark realities of the past."

Judge D'Army Bailey led the 1983 effort to save the motel with the Lorraine Civil Rights Museum Foundation. After raising sufficient funds to purchase the Lorraine Motel on the Courthouse steps at an auction, plans by designers Jerry Eisterhold and Benjamin lawless were used for the transformation to the National Civil Rights Museum.

The museum was dedicated on Independence Day, July 4, 1991. Among the 6,000 present were the Rev. Joseph Lowery, Rosa Parks, the Rev. Jesse Jackson, actors Morgan Freeman, Blair Underwood and Cybill Shepherd, and then Governor of Arkansas William Jefferson 'Bill' Clinton. Doves were released into the air, and Bailey and Rosa Parks shared the duty of cutting the red, white and blue ribbon that officially opened the new Museum.

Benjamin Lawless, Jerry Eisterhold.

Gerard Eisterhold has been president, principal designer and project director of Eisterhold Associates Incorporated (EAI) since its inception in 1980. His expertise includes interactive technology and its application in an interpretive environment. Civil Rights projects that EAI have completed include the National Civil Rights Museum in Memphis; the International Civil Rights Center & Museum in Greensboro, North Carolina; the Rosa Parks Museum and the Rosa Parks Children's Wing, and the Civil Rights Memorial Center in Montgomery. EAI projects also include the Southern Poverty Law Center, the Department of the Interior and Federal Reserve Banks, and Truman Presidential Museum. Benjamin Lawless worked with Eisterhold Associates Inc., (EAI) from 1984 until his death in 2013.

Judge Bailey posing with a model of the Lorraine Motel and National Civil Rights Center.

Hadassah Leiberman, wife of Senator Joe Leiberman, points to Bailey's designation as Founder on plaque at entry to Museum.

Adrienne Bailey, Muhammad Ali and Judge Bailey at a National Civil Rights Museum reception at the Bailey home, presenting Ali a promotional video on Museum plans.

Coretta Scott King at opening banquet during dedication of Museum.

Cybil Shepard, Rosa Parks, Blair Underwood, Judge Bailey, Ben Hooks, Billy Kyles and Jesse
   Jackson, at dedication of Museum.

H. Rap Brown at Civil Rights symposium during dedication of Museum.

Judge Bailey speaking at the
Museum Groundbreaking
ceremony.

Museum groundbreaking, Rev. Ralph Abernathy looks at balcony of Lorraine Motel.

Rev. Joseph Lowery of SCLC arriving for Museum dedication, July 3rd.

Rosa Parks gets first look at Montgomery bus boycott
exhibit during Museum dedication.

Famed civil rights lawyers Arthur Kinoy and William Kunstler during Museum
dedication symposium.

The successful effort by D'Army Bailey to transform the Lorraine Motel into the National Civil Rights Museum can be said to be a natural outgrowth of his many years of engagement on the front lines of social change. During these years, he was exposed to the thinking of others in a way that expanded his knowledge of the Civil Rights landscape, and Bailey used this information in practice of direct action, as he later recounted in his biography.

As a college student, Bailey attended the 1960 Congress of the National Student Association (NSA), with students from around the country, to include then NSA President-elect Tom Hayden, who would become a prominent peace activist, and Barney Frank, a young man who broke segregation law by drinking from a 'colored only' water fountain during a trip to South Carolina, participated in Freedom Summer in 1964, and led financial reform as a member of the US House of Representatives. Bailey participated in another NSA in 1961, led by Agnes Scott College alumna Constance Currie and SNCC member Bob Zellner from Mobile, Alabama. He gained knowledge as well from Professor Adolph Reed Sr., who encouraged progressivism and critical thinking in Bailey and other students, but also in his son and namesake, Dr. Adolph Reed, Jr., one of America's foremost progressive scholars. By 1962, Bailey had joined a student organization at Southern University which received funding support from the Congress of Racial Equality (CORE), meeting on March 24, 1962 with Student Nonviolent Coordinating Committee (SNCC) workers James Forman, Julian Bond, John Lewis and Ella Baker, to strategize on expanding the Movement across the South.

On Independence Day, 1963, Bailey headed up DARE (Direct Action for Racial Equality), the Washington DC project of the Northern Student Movement founded by Peter Countryman. DARE, along with CORE, SNCC, NAACP and 40 other church, labor, political and peace organizations held a mass demonstration at Gwynn Oak Amusement Park in Towson, Maryland, a public park which barred blacks from entering. Bailey was among 200 protestors arrested and locked into the Baltimore county jail and courtroom, which served as an overflow. Among those arrested was a young man referred to by Bailey as 'Mickey' Schwerner, a New Yorker participating in his first civil rights protest'. Michael Schwerner, along with Andrew Goodman and James Chaney, would be murdered in Meridian, Mississippi in 1964. His desire to remain engaged in activism led him to choose a career in law.

After completing his law degree, Bailey practiced in San Francisco, and served on the Berkeley, California, City Council from 1971 to 1973. He returned to Memphis in 1974, where he opened a law practice with his brother, Walter Lee Bailey, Jr. In 1990, he was elected to the position of Circuit Court Judge. Bailey joined Wilkes & McHugh, P.A. after retiring from his position as a Circuit Court Judge in Memphis, Tennessee. Judge Bailey was a member of the Tennessee Bar Association, the Arkansas Bar Association and State Bar of California. He lectured at several law schools, appeared as a guest analyst on Court TV, and published legal articles in scholarly journals at the law schools of the University of Toledo, Washington and Lee, Howard, and Harvard. He passed away on July 12, 2015, with the good he built continuing to have a powerful social contribution.

Medgar Evers House

As film director Rob Reiner's *Ghosts of Mississippi* depicted the aftermath of the assassination of Mississippi NAACP leader Medgar Evers, they incorporated the interiors of the Evers house, including the driveway and bedrooms. But it was not without emotional cost to members of the crew. Even Reiner himself could not stand in that space without being impacted by the weight of what happened there.

Scholar Manning Marable recounted a similar experience:

> *"When Myrlie [Evers-Williams] invited me to visit her former home, I thought I was prepared for what would surely be an emotional experience. Yet no amount of historical study or documentary knowledge could have truly prepared me for the tangible power of past tragedy held in that physical place. Myrlie and I stood in the driveway of their home, where the assassin's bullet had struck Medgar in the back. Kneeling, she softly explained that for months following Medgar's murder she would go outside in the dark of the night and vigorously attempt to scrub the blood-stains off the driveway. No matter how hard she scrubbed, no matter how many sleepless nights she spent trying, Medgar's bloodstains would not come clean. Her plaintive words were almost apologetic: She had been unable to wipe clean a stain that had left her without a loving husband and her children without a father. I was so overwhelmed I could barely keep from weeping aloud."*

Bronze statue of Evers at the Medgar Evers Boulevard Library, Jackson, Mississippi, 2013.

Physical connection with the house in Jackson, Mississippi uniquely conveyed, then and now, information about the violent tenor of the Civil Rights movement.

Seventeen years after the film, hundreds gathered in Jackson on June 11, 2013 for the 50th Commemoration of the Evers assassination. Myrlie Evers-Williams, Evers' widow, and Ben Jealous, both fresh from their National NAACP leadership roles, participated in wreath laying ceremony at the Evers House, along with Former President Bill Clinton and Attorney General Eric Holder, Mississippi Governor Phil Bryant, and President Barack Obama. Despite the presence of these luminaries, the ongoing work on the Medgar and Myrlie Evers Institute and the broad press coverage of commemoration activities, Medgar Evers has a conflicted status in Civil Rights movement history.

Many in the general population have not heard of Evers, have little knowledge of his contributions to civil rights, and are unaware that his contributions to the field of communications were part of the civil rights struggle. The restoration and interpretation of his home is an important component in doing the good work of filling that civil rights information gap.

While Evers is widely recognized by historians and other scholars for his organizing efforts with the Mississippi NAACP, and for his murder, a civil rights watershed event described by many as a martyrdom, Evers is missing from such seminal African American anthologies as the late historian Manning Marable's *Let Nobody Turn Us Around: Voices of Resistance, Reform and Renewal.* Major literary and scholarly works on his life did not emerge until the late 1990's, and within the last ten years, decades after his murder. During the height of the 2013 commemoration, descriptions in the Washington Post emphasized the importance of inclusion of Evers' name in the civil rights pantheon. The focus on recognition is appropriate, with the general public still largely unaware of the man and his actions, as one visitor to the Medgar Evers House told a journalist: "High school students learn about Rosa Parks and Martin Luther King Jr., but little else."

The release of recent historical literature and the digitization of older source material invite new questions about Evers' life and work. Michael Vinson Williams, whose dissertation became the book, "Medgar Wiley Evers: Mississippi Martyr" in 2011 noted that it is 'certain that his work and life deserve deeper examination in order to fully understand his contribution to the struggle for social equality". Historian Ronald Bailey emphasizes that Medgar Evers is a key to understanding the Civil Rights movement in the South, in Mississippi, and within the United States. Judge D'Army Bailey, leader of the Lorraine Motel restoration, experienced the November 22, 1964 assassination of

President John F. Kennedy against the backdrop of the murder of Evers in Jackson the year before, and in context of the violence that all who participated in civil rights protests risked and endured.

Evers, born in Decatur, Mississippi in 1925, walked miles to complete his high school education, and joined local civil rights efforts after serving in the US Army and fighting in World War II. He began working with his wife Myrlie to establish local NAACP chapters throughout the Delta area of Mississippi in 1951. In 1954 his unsuccessful attempt to integrate the University of Mississippi Law School was noticed by the National NAACP. That year, Medgar and his family moved to Jackson, Mississippi, where he set up the NAACP headquarters, and began investigate alleged crimes against blacks. Evers officially became NAACP Field Secretary in January 1955.   Historian Michael Williams noted, "the NAACP relied upon Medgar to investigate instances of abuse, physical, verbal, or otherwise, against the African American populace in Mississippi. As a result, he investigated charges of police brutality, murder, voter discrimination, economic sanctions against African Americans, and a host of other injustices.   Evers translated racial attacks as personal assaults against the integrity of African Americans, and he refused to allow such attacks to go unchallenged."

Today's viewers of WLBT-TV, the NBC affiliate in Jackson, Mississippi, may be unaware that during the 1950s, the station owners at that time participated in a common practice of television stations in the South: switching to another network when shows featuring blacks aired. WLBT-TV ran the graphic, 'Sorry, cable trouble,' over a dark screen when network news reports of civil rights protests, or Dr. King's address in Washington were televised. The graphic stayed until the news event was over. In 1954, however, Medgar Evers challenged the station, and led the Jackson chapter of the

NAACP to file a complaint about these practices to the Federal Communications Commission (FCC), according to scholar Michele Himes.

When WLBT-TV received a network program featuring an interview by Thurgood Marshall, then general counsel of the NAACP, the general manager rejected the program, electing instead to substitute a 'Sorry, Cable trouble" sign. The NAACP's Washington office 'got word of the incident', and sent a letter on November 16, 1957 to FCC Chair John C. Doerfer, according to Historian John Mills.

Future American Supreme Court justice Thurgood Marshall, then an attorney for the NAACP. Source: US News & World Report Collection, Library of Congress, 1957.

1957: The Little Rock Crisis

In 1957, WLBT-TV carried a program entitled, 'The Little Rock Crisis', highlighting education challenges in Little Rock, Arkansas. Panelists included white Mississippi US congressman James Eastland, who spoke in favor of segregation. No black advocate, nor any other presenter of alternative opinions was included in the television program. Evers and the Mississippi NAACP brought evidence to the Federal Communications Commission that WLBT-TV and other southern television stations refused time to civil rights organizations, while airing the weekly syndicated discussion program produced by the White Citizens' Council, described by scholar Michele Hilmes as 'virulently racist' and 'pro-segregation". Evers' letter, dated October 17, 1957, sent to the Chairman of the FCC charged that the station was presenting only the 'segregationist point of view'. Although Williams argues in his dissertation that the Fairness Doctrine supported Evers' demands, the FCC declined to hear the case until WLBT-TV's scheduled license renewal hearing in 1958. Evers changed his approach, opting to contact members of the broadcast industry directly. He asked NBC anchor Dave Garroway for an opportunity to appear on the Today show. Evers' objective was to offset the 'distorted and slanted story' of race relations in Mississippi produced by Governor Coleman 'and other southern whites'. Both of these efforts failed; in 1959, the FCC dismissed the complaints and renewed WLBT-TV's license for seven more years.

1961: The Candidate and the FCC

In 1961, Rev. Robert L.T. Smith became the first African American man to run for Congress in Mississippi since Reconstruction. WLBT-TV refused to sell Smith airtime for his campaign. Smith, Evers, and local civil rights groups sent petitions to the FCC citing Fairness Doctrine violations, claiming that the station publicized White citizens' council activities, allowing 'racist and

REV. R. L. T. SMITH
CANDIDATE FOR
CONGRESS
3RD DISTRICT
GIVE MISSISSIPPI A LIFT
VOTE FOR
SMITH
1072 LYNCH STREET. Room 16. FL 5-7224 CAMPAIGN HEADQUARTERS

Campaign materials for Rev. Robert L.T. Smith.

segregationists groups ample time on local television, while denying and suppressing comparable publicity for civil rights advocates.' Evers was quoted in the newspapers as saying: 'Ethics of the Federal Communications Commission will require it. Whether public service time or paid time, our interest is in getting time." Evers announced in 1963 that the NAACP was 'going to insist upon having this time because we were attacked by Mayor Thompson", according to Jackson Daily News.

President John F. Kennedy with Outgoing Chairman of the Federal Communications Commission, Newton Minow, and Family, May 1963.

Newton N. Minow, Chairman of the Federal Communications Commission between March 2, 1961 - June 1, 1963, recounted receiving a phone call from former First Lady Eleanor Roosevelt, whom he first met through his law partner Adlai Stevenson, and again when he started his chairmanship of the agency in 1961. Her question: "Why aren't you doing anything to help Reverend Smith?" Minow stated that he was not aware that Rev. Smith and his campaign manager, state NAACP President Aaron Henry, had written to the FCC, receiving no answers. Mrs. Roosevelt reported that the station's response to Henry's request to buy airtime was "Nigger, are you crazy? Get out of here. We're not going to sell you any time." Reverend Smith later reported, when making the same request, the response: that if Smith appeared on WLBT-TV, "they would find my body floating upside down in the river."

Photograph of Senator John F. Kennedy (right) with Allen C. Thompson (center), Mayor of Jackson, Mississippi at a meeting of the American Municipal Association held in Denver, Colorado. Papers of John F. Kennedy. Pre-Presidential Papers. Presidential Campaign Files, 1960. Campaigns by State: Pre-Convention Political Files, 1960. Photo. By: Ralph H. Hargrove; Identification Bureau, Police Department, Jackson, Mississippi.

Minow intervened with FCC staff, who initially agreed with the station that if one candidate did not buy air time, the other candidate could not be on the air so that both would be 'treated equally'. Minow sent a telegram to WLBT-TV asking them to explain and defend their position, which resulted in an attorney for the station responding that Smith would be allowed to buy campaign time and appear on the station. Henry, in later interviews, recalled how the appearance of Reverend Smith on WLBT-TV was a victory for the Black community. Myrlie Evers Williams noted that 'seeing Reverend Smith on television was like the lifting of a giant curtain. He was saying things that had never before been said by a Negro to whites in Mississippi.' While the accounts of this incident do not include Medgar Evers' activism in this case specifically, it can be surmised that Smith, described as an 'NAACP activist' and Henry, who was president of the Mississippi NAACP, benefitted from Evers' guidance due to their ongoing relationship through his role as Jackson NAACP Field Secretary, and his previous experiences interacting with the Federal Communications Commission.

The Challenges Bear Fruit

On May 13, 1963, Jackson, Mississippi Mayor Allen C. Thompson defended race relations in Jackson on radio station WJDX and on WLBT-TV. Thompson defended Jackson as a great city, with beautiful amenities and facilities, and no slums. He bade 'nigra citizens to realize the good they were afforded by living in a progressive city: 'You live in a city where you can work, where you can make a comfortable living. You are treated, no matter what anybody else tells you, with dignity, courtesy and respect.'

Evers 'insisted on equal television time to respond to claims presented by Mayor Allen Thompson, which the activist called an 'attack on the movement for equality', resting on Thompson's rosy outlook on race relations and African Americans' sociopolitical position within the city, a perception that had gone out across the nation, according to the Jackson Daily News. Jackson and the state of

Medgar Evers, state NAACP field secretary, speaks about race relations during a television broadcast, May 20, 1963. AP.

Mississippi, meanwhile, were experiencing increased attention from the national NAACP, due to the city's refusal to pursue school integration. On May 20th, under federal pressure, WLBT-TV allowed Evers onto the airwaves to deliver an editorial on a local news program. Hilmes notes that 'this was the first time an outspoken message had been seen and heard on Jackson airwaves on the topic of ending segregation and denial of rights to African Americans in Mississippi.'

Historian Michael Williams concurred: "At this point, the station felt compelled to grant airtime because, as the historian Stephen Classen has written, WLBT-TV "was sensing the watchful eye of federal regulators" already investigating the station for bias and soliciting comments regarding its coverage and reporting of the admission of James Meredith to the University of Mississippi. Safety concerns made it necessary for Evers's response not to be broadcast live but taped at a secret location and then aired on Jackson station WLBT-TV, according to Williams. Three weeks after this broadcast, on June 12th, Evers was shot and killed in the driveway of his Jackson home. Hilmes notes that 'perhaps motivated by local events', in July 1963, the FCC issued a public notice confirming that a balanced presentation of racial issues was required under Fairness Doctrine guidelines.

Activities Post-Evers' Death

Viewing information and civil rights through the "Montgomery to Memphis" lens, some scholars emphasize the role of media during the civil rights movement as contributing to awareness through coverage, creating a substantial shift in racial attitudes of whites toward blacks. In this view, communication is a tool used to bring attention to the Movement's agenda items of desegregation and an end to racialized violence. Research scientist Reynolds Farley cites Gunnar Myrdal's 1944's *American Dilemma* as the launch of awareness of the systematic denial of the rights of Blacks in the South. Farley notes that despite this and a series of groundbreaking events leading up to *Brown vs. Board of Education*, it was necessary to have national attention focused on the civil rights grievance of blacks. Nationally televised events, such as the 1955 killing of Emmett Till in Mississippi, and the 1956

Montgomery bus boycott, led by Dr. King, provided extensive coverage that helped whites in other parts of the country realize in full the racial issues in the South.

The Civil Rights movement helped the broader public to see these inequities, and helped the nation to see the disparity between national norms, laws and principles and the violence of Southern whites against blacks, according to journalists Gene Roberts and Hank Klibanoff. Farley notes that front page newspaper and TV coverage of the following events helped to accomplish the success of the civil rights movement. Farley also noted the new norms of racial and gender diversity that had developed over time, citing examples of President George W. Bush's appointment of a diverse cabinet, diversity on corporation boards, and in administrative jobs.

The communications issues of *portrayal, coverage and content*, differ from *issues of media control*, and a civil rights agenda emphasizing the necessity of that control to bring about the empowerment of Black people in America. These portrayal norms are 'inclusion' norms, as opposed to norms that more specifically address Black self-actualization, self- articulation, pro-active capacity, and self-empowerment. This distinction is also suggested by such terminology as 'window-dressing.'

Local volunteers in Jackson began a covert operation of monitoring television stations' output, keeping records of fairness violations. According to legal scholar Robert Horwitz, between 1956 and 1957, Dr. Martin Luther King Jr. met with northern church leaders during the Montgomery bus boycott, and complained to leaders of Congregational Christian Board of Home Missions of terrible treatment blacks were receiving on southern radio and television. The Rev. Everett C. Parker, Director of the Office of Communication of the United Church of Christ, was part of these meetings.

In April 1964, the United Church of Christ (UCC) and local citizens filed a number of petitions to deny renewal of WLBT-TV's station license to the FCC. In 1965 FCC staff recommended WLBT-TV's license be temporarily denied so that hearings could be held, issuing a one year probationary approval and declined to hold hearings. In March 1966, The UCC appealed this decision, and the US Court of Appeals found in their favor, revoking WLBT-TV's license, according to FCC records.

In May 1967, FCC began formal hearings on WLBT-TV's license in Jackson. In 1968, the FCC ruled to approve renewal. UCC appealed and the Court reversed the decision, ordering a comparative renewal process to begin. In June 1971, a decision to turn operation of the station over to an interim organization was made. In December 1979, the FCC awarded WLBT-TV's station license to a group organized by local citizen advocates, with 51 percent black ownership.

Arthur S. Fleming, Chairman, US Commission on Civil Rights 1974-1981.

Organizations concerned with racial and ethnic representation complained to the FCC, broadcasters, and the general public. In 1977, the US Commission on Civil Rights published, "Window Dressing on the Set: Women and Minorities in Television." Findings were that US news organizations had done a poor job of integrating nonwhite, female reporters, producers and managers into their news operations. National Black Media Coalition, the National Black Media Producers Association, and Black Effort for Soul in Television (BEST) 'consolidated the gains that African Americans were beginning to make in national media, advocating for more.'

While Everett Parker clearly is responsible for engaging the UCC in the lawsuit, the groundwork laid by Medgar Evers in his repeated attempts to change communication practice in his city left a paper trail that arguably could have led Parker to choose Jackson and WLBT-TV as the test case. While earlier interviews stated that the inspiration for the lawsuit came from a conversation that Parker had with Rev. Dr. Martin Luther King Jr. at a meeting with King, Andrew Young and Parker, according to scholar Robert Horwitz, later interviews showed uncertainty. Historian Kay Mills stated, "So many years later, it is difficult to date this meeting. Parker remembers that it occurred perhaps as early as 1956-1957, the date cited by Horwitz' 'Broadcast Reform Revisited', or perhaps as late as 1961." The Rev. Jesse Jackson credits the inspiration of the UCC communications case to Dr. King.

This connection is understandable both times, since in the popular mind, Dr. Martin Luther King equals the Civil Rights movement, and the best way to clarify the connection between the UCC communications case and the civil rights movement is to attach it to Dr. King. But an additional connection emerges from examination of the FCC paper trail that Medgar Evers brought into being before his untimely death, and the attention that WLBT-TV received, ranging from FCC staff coming personally to Jackson, and from the FCC chair intervening personally in the Smith airtime case.

Among Evers' Good Works: Civil Rights Information

Information and communication were vital components in the expansion of rights for blacks; after the assassinations of King and Kennedy, the Kerner Report pinpointed communication as a significant area that would provide redress and opportunities for blacks. The National Advisory Commission on Civil Disorders, launched by President Lyndon B. Johnson on July 28, 1967, tasked Otto

Governor Otto Kerner (center) meeting with Roy Wilkins (left) and President Lyndon B. Johnson (right) at the White House in 1967. Source: Lyndon Baines Johnson Library.

Kerner, Governor of Illinois, to chair the group, and provide some level of understanding and remedies concerning the riots and protests in Newark, Detroit, and other communities in the summer of 1967. The Kerner Commission Report was produced in March 1968. The chief observation of the Commission is what Massey calls "'American Apartheid,' two communities that for all intents and purposes were becoming two societies: one black and one white," according to works by Douglas Massey and Nancy A. Denton.

Listed as a 'Second Level of Intensity' in the 1968 Kerner Commission Report on Civil Unrest is 'ineffectiveness of the political structure and grievance mechanisms.' Remedies to this problem were found in a chapter dedicated to the News Media, and questions raised by the President about the effect that mass media may have had on the riots. The results were drawn from efforts by the Commission including a national conference of industry leaders, quantitative analysis of riot coverage, and qualitative interviews. A summary of the Kerner Commission report indicated that the failures of the news media to 'accurately portray the scale and character of the violence', as well as underlying causes and consequences of the event were based on low performance norms with regard to the 'Negro ghettos' overall, and required industry correction. Specific recommendations to the media included recruitment of blacks into journalism, provision of training, and the establishment of the

'Institute of Urban Communication, a privately organized and funded organization tasked with recruiting and training black journalists.

In 1997 the Rainbow-PUSH Coalition filed petitions contesting the transfer of four Washington DC radio stations from Viacom International to the Evergreen Corporation. Inner City Press/Communicate the Move filed petitions against the transfer of two New York radio stations from Viacom to Evergreen. Rainbow filed a Petition for Special Relief, asking to deny transfer. It sought this relief because it alleged that Viacom failed to keep a promise it made in 1994 pledging to 'an affirmative action effort to increase the possibility of purchase of one of both stations by a minority-controlling entity." The settlement between Viacom, Evergreen and Chancellor and the Rainbow Push Coalition included the following stipulations:

> *"Viacom, Evergreen and Chancellor agreed to spend two million dollars to enhance opportunities for minority participation in broadcasting. This included providing $400,000 for three studies on minority broadcast ownership to be conducted at independent universities, providing $600,000 for a broadcast education and advocacy fund to conduct public education and advocacy on the subject of minority media entrepreneurs, proving $800,000 administered by independent trustee David Dinkins, former Mayor of New York City, for a series of conferences that would focus on teaching the public about the value of minority media entrepreneurs; $80,000 in scholarships to the African American Media Incubator, a nonprofit Washington-based broadcast training school. As a result of this settlement, the Rainbow petition was withdrawn."*

Jesse Jackson speaks on a radio broadcast from the headquarters of Operation PUSH, (People United to Save Humanity) at its annual convention. July 1973.

Jesse Jackson's work, part of this extension of the civil rights movement, stepped onto the path of communication activism that Evers had forged, making it part of his institution's mission. According to their website, The Rainbow/PUSH Coalition is a 'multi-racial, multi-issue, international membership for social, racial and economic justice organization founded by Rev. Jesse L. Jackson, Sr. The Coalition was a merger between the National Rainbow Coalition, founded in 1965, and Operation Push, founded in 1971. Rev. Jackson's history with the American civil rights movement began with his appointment by Dr. Martin Luther King, Jr. to run the Southern Christian Leadership Council's program, 'Operation Breadbasket in Chicago in the 1960's. The organization lists among its accomplishments, "challenging broadcast station licenses to ensure equal employment opportunities in the media, lobbying to include more minorities in all areas of the entertainment industry, and negotiating economic covenants with major corporations, resulting in hundreds of minority owned franchises."

While the NAACP leadership and other black local leadership were satisfied to issue statements, it was Evers who made demands for 'equal time', citing FCC rules. A difference between 'civil rights leaders understanding the power of television, and using it to project images of their cause to a worldwide audience,' Michele Hilmes believes that by the 1970s, when the case as resolved, a new era

144

in 'broadcasting had begun, in which all power of television representation did not belong in white hands, and in which no station could have prevented the mere exposure of black voices and faces in a local market the way that WLBT-TV had. She concludes that, "It is likely that even if WLBT-TV had retained its former ownership, its broadcasting practices would have changed with the times as well."

In Ms. Hilmes' view, the significance of the FCC final decision in this case is that the FCC was forced "to recognize the voice of the citizens in its renewal process...a process in which citizens were granted legal standing." Previously only corporate competitors were given this standing, and only their voices could be heard in the renewal process. The FCC had 'opened the door' to more direct community involvement and potentially, community impact. Making this fight direct, and taking it to the Federal Communications Commission, according to scholar Hugh Torres, was one of the lynchpin actions that allowed blacks great access to media resources.

While Mississippi press editors and publishers defended segregation, Evers played a major role in civil rights movement. His presence in one of the country's most racist states provided other civil rights organizers with an example of personal strength and fortitude unmatched in the late 1950s and early 1960s.

After Evers' death, the agenda expanded further into communication, to include media education and training for African Americans. One of today's major civil rights figures, the Rev. Jesse Jackson, Jr., personifies this media-oriented shift and broadening of the agenda, influenced in part by Medgar Evers. The work of civil rights activists today is influenced as much by Evers as they are by such luminaries as Dr. Martin Luther King Jr.

Media scholar Steven Classen concluded that the changes in Mississippi television were created by the interaction of interdependent actions of local activists, reform groups, and federal jurists. He describes Evers activism as focused on 'access to broadcast outlets, motivated by a desire to more frequently and publicly connect black voices to ongoing debates and social crises concerning voting, educational opportunity, and public employment.'

Evers was connected directly and explicitly to the civil rights movement through his professional role with the NAACP. It is significant that he fought for the right for black voices to be heard, just as he fought for other civil rights issues of inclusion in general society. It is this that sets him apart from other civil rights leaders at the time. Information and Communications became part of the Civil Rights agenda, through the efforts of Civil Rights leadership. Evers' appearance alone signaled an interruption in what journalist Kay Mills described as "an especially effective blackout of African Americans on southern TV stations." African American civil rights activists wanted the influential medium of television to provide impartial coverage on issues of importance to the black community. Williams and Mills agree that by the 1960s, blacks were engaged in a concerted effort "to challenge the rules governing television and the inertia of the agency charged with enforcing them, the Federal Communications Commission." The critical role of social media in political change today demonstrate the advantage that access to information and the ability to communicate have created formidable social change agents.

Strengthening Medgar Evers House Capacity for Good

In honor of the 50th Anniversary of the March on Washington in 2013, CBS News ran a story on ten civil rights landmarks identified by the National Trust for Historic Preservation. Five of these sites were considered by the Trust to be endangered: the Medgar Evers House was on that list.

Minnie White Watson.

After the assassination, Myrlie Evers and her children moved to California, leaving the Medgar Evers house and its memories behind. In February 1993, the year of the 30th Anniversary of Evers' slaying, Evers' widow donated the House to Tougaloo College. According to *Jet magazine*, Tougaloo was 'the cradle of civil rights activities' in the area, because activists could gather there without fear. Tougaloo hired Minnie White Watson in 1997 to lead its transformation and development. "People need to know the things he did, the things he stood for, the things he died for," Watson said in an interview with the *Jackson Free Press*. This motivates her in her work at the Evers House.

Raymond Arsenault, left, and Minnie White Watson, center, listen to a presenter at the Sustainers consortium.

In 1995-1996 a restoration with funding from the Mississippi State Legislature was completed, including interpretation of interiors with such detail that the mattresses in the children's room were placed on the floor, out of range of shots through the windows in case of an assassination attempt. After this renovation, serious destabilizing conditions caused the house to close for a few years. Mrs. White put in more than a decade of work, generating over $225,000 in grants and other supports to make critical major restorations to the site, including mildew treatment, roof replacement and correction of sagging and deteriorated floors.

WFT Architects was contracted lead the team that conducted the site assessment and complete the restoration. They used photographs produced by Myrlie Evers; reviewed newsreel footage and news articles, and conducted interviews with black entrepreneurs Winston J. Thompson and Leroy Burnett, who designed the first African American subdivision in 1956. With the completion of the restoration, the house was opened to the public for tours in time for Monday, June 10, 2013, the 50th anniversary of Medgar's assassination. The Medgar Evers House was a recipient of the 2014 Heritage Awards for Restoration from the Mississippi Heritage Trust.

A rededication ceremony for the house reopening after renovations was attended by over 100 guests, and featured a speech by Rena Evers-Everette, the daughter of Medgar Evers, who was eight years old when her father was assassinated. 'When I'm here, the spirit of Dad is protecting us', said Evers-Everette. Her remarks, and those of others present, reflected the central focus that drives the ongoing protection and restoration of this sacred space:

> *"The Rev. Larry L. Johnson, the Tougaloo College chaplain, said the ceremony Monday was more than the rededication of a home. It is a time for us to rededicate ourselves to the cause of freedom and justice for all people because we know all people are part of the family of God," Johnson said.*

Watson serves as assistant archivist and curator of the Medgar Wiley Evers Historic (House) Museum and registrar for the Tougaloo Art Colony at Tougaloo College. Her professional career includes Program Assistant/Payroll Officer for the Southern Association of Community Health Center (SACHC); and Assistant to the Executive Director of Economic Development Corporation at Tougaloo College. Ms. Watson is a community activist, serving as board member of the Bailey Avenue Renewal Coalition, a group charged with revitalizing its main community corridors, including the historic Medgar Evers Boulevard; and the Hinds County Human Resource Agency. She is also a member of the National

Council of Negro Women; National Association for the Advancement of Colored People (NAACP), and Educators United for Global Awareness.

In an interview for C-Span, Watson talked about the calling that Medgar Evers had to continue his work, despite the danger. The calling to save this house so critical to civil rights history is one that she feels, and shares with others as they opened up the doors to let people flow through, and then made sure the stories are passed on to new generations. It's a personal calling, as Watson met Medgar Evers personally in 1961, when he came to her class at Campbell College to speak to students about the NAACP.

On February 12, 2015 H.R. 959, entitled 'the Medgar Evers House Study Act,' was introduced in Congress by Mississippi Representative Bennie Thompson. The bill would authorize the Secretary of the Interior to conduct a special resource study of Medgar Evers House for the purpose of it ultimately becoming a part of the National Park Service system. The original bill did not make it out of committee, but on September 16, 2015, the rules were suspended and the bill was passed; a Senate version of the bill was introduced in October by Mississippi Senator Thad Cochran. With a hearing held on the two bills in 2016 by the Committee on Energy and Natural Resources subcommittee on National Parks, indications are strong for the future capacity of this historic site to continue doing good, supported by increased status and resources.

Brown AME Chapel, starting point of the Selma to Montgomery March. Opposite: Photographer Francis Mitchell's contact sheet showing Malcolm X and others addressing audience at Brown Chapel, Selma, February 4, 1965.

Selma to Montgomery Trail

Southern Christian Leadership Conference (SCLC) leader Rev. James Bevel had an epiphany. He was speaking at the funeral of Jimmie Lee Jackson, who had been shot in the stomach at a Selma, Alabama voter registration protest on February 18, 1965 while trying to protect his mother and grandfather from being assaulted. Bevel had a vision of the people 'going to see the king,' taking Jackson's body and laying their demands for justice and grievances down before him, as Esther had done in the Bible.

The roiling waves that started this epiphany have been documented by scholars, participants and observers to their source back in the 1920s, with the birth of the Dallas County Voters' League (DCVL). Sam and Amelia Boynton had taken up leadership of the League in the 1950's, and began reaching out for assistance outside the state in the 1960s. In November 1962 the Voter Education Project of the Southern Regional Council sent Bernard Lafayette of the Student Nonviolent Coordinating Committee (SNCC) to assist local efforts to register voters. The death of Sam Boynton in May 1963 led to a memorial service and massive voter rights rally with SNCC speaker James Forman, and a sharp increase in protests and rallies afterward. On September 15th of that year, four girls were killed in the Sixteenth Street Baptist Church bombing in Birmingham, and a planned Student Nonviolent Coordinating Committee, Dallas County Improvement Association and Dallas County Voters League rally in Selma for the next day led to sit-ins, protests and rallies with increasing numbers of participants and escalating violent response from police. By July 1964, only the Courageous Eight, including Amelia Boynton, continued to meet in the face of a Court injunction.

Locals contacted the Southern Christian Leadership Council (SCLC) and invited their participation. In December SCLC announced plans that brought thousands of people to participate. By January 1965, SCLC, SNCC and local groups were working together, and activists came from around the country, including Malcolm X, who spoke at a mass meeting at Brown Chapel AME. Shortly after this, both Malcolm X and Jimmie Lee Jackson were dead.

Cornerstone of Brown Chapel AME Church, Selma Alabama.

Monument on the grounds of Brown AME Chapel, Selma, Alabama.

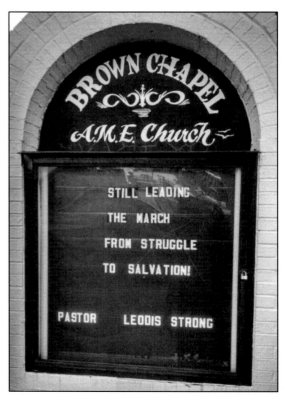

Marquee, Brown Chapel AME church, Selma Alabama 2015.

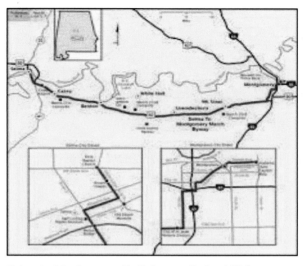

Selma to Montgomery Trail. Source: Federal Highway Administration.

Bevel spoke of the idea in Selma's Brown Chapel A.M.E. Church, and SCLC developed a plan for a march from Selma to Montgomery, the state's capital, to meet with Governor George Wallace. On March 7, 1965, the marchers, including John Lewis, Amelia Boynton, SNCC's Bob Moses, Hosea Williams, Albert Turner and others met at Brown Chapel and started their walk, not expecting the attack that would come. The protesters were met by a wall of blue at the foot of the Pettus Bridge. Policemen charged the protesters with clubs and tear gas, putting marchers in retreat:

"The officers showed no mercy or discretion, beating everyone they could, including women, children and reporters. Boynton, Foster and Lewis, along with a score of others, lay unconscious or vomiting."

ABC news interrupted its airing of 'Judgment at Nuremberg' to report on the events of 'Bloody Sunday.'

The March 9th attempt was larger, with the crowd of protesters swelled by viewers who had watched the beatings on television. SCLC was reluctant, because moving forward with the march would mean defying a court order, but SNCC was ready to move forward. The march, with more than two thousand participants, reached the Pettus Bridge, but was turned around voluntarily by Rev. Dr. Martin Luther King Jr., shortly before completing the bridge crossing, to the consternation of many followers and observers.

The day did not end without violent retribution: three white clergymen who had answered Dr. King's call for clergy of all faiths and races to participate in the march were attacked. Rev. James Reeb received the worst of the attack, his skull fractured with a baseball bat, and he died two days later. Reeb, a native of Kansas and Casper, Wyoming, became a Unitarian Minister assigned to a church in Washington, DC. He allowed the group DARE (Direct Action for Racial Equality) to use his church for community classrooms as one of his early efforts to support social change. A leader of DARE, D'Army Bailey, who would later lead the transformation of the Lorraine Hotel where Dr. Martin Luther King was assassinated, traveled from law school in Boston to speak at the memorial rally for Rev. Reeb, organized by the Worchester Student Movement on the Clark University campus on March 15, 1965. Dr. Martin Luther King, Jr. delivered a eulogy for Reeb at Brown Memorial Chapel on that same day in Selma. Reeb's murder provoked a national response, and increased focus on the struggle in Selma.

The third and final march on March 16th reflected the determination to make it to Montgomery. With a five day schedule, marchers left Selma five thousand strong – religious leaders, Catholic, Jews, Black and White, Asian and Native American walked together with march leaders down Highway 80. In the first row was Dr. King and his wife Coretta Scott, John Lewis, Hosea Williams, Andrew Young, A. Philip Randolph, Ralph Abernathy and Dick Gregory. In the next row was the local leadership: Amelia Boynton, Marie Foster and Frederick D. (F. D.) Reese. They crossed the bridge shadowed by worldwide press, and without interruption of law enforcement, headed through Lowndes County. After the first seven miles they stopped at David Hill's farm in Dallas County. The next stop was the City of St. Jude, a religious community. The group enjoyed an outdoor concert with performances by Sammy Davis Jr., Joan Baez, Dick Gregory and Peter Paul and Mary.

Awaiting the marchers, downtown Montgomery, Alabama 1965.

On the last day 25,000 marchers arrived in Montgomery, filling the lawn and steps of the State House. On the front lines were Amelia Boynton, Rosa Parks, Dr. Martin Luther King, Jr. and Coretta Scott King, Ralph and Juanita Abernathy, and Dallas County Voter League president F.D. Reese. At this point, Montgomery has become the centerpiece of the struggle; Selma and Montgomery were bookends to a grueling walk with no shortage of menacing witnesses on a mission to strike fear. But the marchers sidestepped any challenges, even their own feelings, finally coming face to face with their state capital building, in order to demand their rights to participate in their governance as full and free equals to the white population.

The first of the Selma to Montgomery marchers. Montgomery, Alabama 1965.

NBC news crew witnesses the final hours of the Selma to Montgomery March. Montgomery, Alabama 1965.

Law enforcement and citizens in the final hours of the Selma to Montgomery March. Montgomery, Alabama 1965.

The bulk of the marchers coming down the street, with police and others looking on. Montgomery, Alabama 1965.

The first of the Selma to Montgomery marchers. Montgomery, Alabama 1965.

Leadership line of the march, bearing flags. Montgomery, Alabama 1965.

The marchers await the speakers, Montgomery, Alabama 1965.

Rosa Parks addresses the marchers in front of the Alabama State House in Montgomery, 1965.

Dr. Martin Luther King speaks, flanked by Rev. C.T. Vivian, Ralph Bunche, among others.

Roy Wilkins speaks; Bayard Rustin, A. Philip Randolph, John Lewis, Coretta and Dr. Martin Luther King seated.

Alongside the victory of safely reaching their destination, and leaders' speeches, the citizens' petition was reluctantly accepted by a member of Governor Wallace's staff. But there would still be sacrifice. On March 25, Viola Liuzzo, who had left her husband and children behind in order to assist with the Selma to Montgomery March, was shot in the head and killed while driving a black male volunteer on Highway 80.

The stretch of Highway 80 where Viola Liuzzo was murdered.

Until her death in 2015, Amelia Boynton Robinson returned annually to the trail between the two cities to participate in the Bridge Jubilee, to once again be on hallowed ground. Other activists who return regularly to the Selma to Montgomery Trail include Andrew Young, who played a lead role in organizing the original March. Folk singer Joan Baez, civil rights leader C.T. Vivian and activist Diane Nash put their boots on the ground in 1965, and in years since. Harry Belafonte, asked by Dr. King to bring artists into the movement, is one for whom the Selma struggles are cast in future tense: "Civil rights is a constant." Belafonte remarked in 2013. "It's never of the past, it's with you all the time. " Tony Bennett, one of the first artists Belafonte called, appeared in the miniseries 'King', returned to Selma to see some of the changes the March led to, and sang at the 50th Anniversary of the "I have a dream speech'. The hallowed spaces were there to receive him.

Cast of the film 'Selma' visit Selma, Alabama on King Day. Director Ava Duvernay and actor David Oyelowo pictured.

The spaces of the famous Alabama march for liberation are prominently featured in the 2014 Paramount Pictures release 'Selma', directed by Ava DuVernay and produced by Oprah Winfrey's Harpo Productions, Plan B Entertainment, with co-Presidents Jeremy Kleiner and Dede Gardner and owner Brad Pitt, and Pathé, with producers Cameron McCracken and Christian Coulson. In a sense, the spaces themselves are the story, with principal

Women religious in the audience listening to Selma cast and crew speak on King Day 2015.

photography shot in Montgomery and Selma, Alabama. The film represents the first film and the third dramatization of the Selma to Montgomery March; the first, the television miniseries 1978, 'King', included the march, but focused primarily on the life of the Rev. Dr. Martin Luther King, Jr. The second was 'Selma, Lord, Selma', airing on ABC in 1999, telling the story through the eyes of a young girl.

The streets of Selma filled during a re-enactment of the March to the Pettus Bridge by Selma cast and crew.

Barbara Tagger at Harriet Tubman Underground Railroad National Monument unveiling.

In addition to highlighting the role of Martin Luther King Jr., at this pivotal time in his career, the Paramount film features dramatizations of Selma leaders like Amelia Boynton Robinson, who was beaten on the Trail by police, yet continued with the march to its triumphant end at the State House in Montgomery. The capacity to film the sequence of events, and painstakingly reconstruct the March where it took place, is one of the fruits of preserving Selma to Montgomery as a National Historic Trail. Location assistant Leif Tilden spoke of days spent at Selma sites to 'get the feel and vibe and put the story together', choosing the Edmund Pettus Bridge and Brown Chapel AME Church, Trail sites for inclusion in the film.

The combination of the film, the sacred sites it used, and the occasion of the 50th Anniversary of the March drew more than 100,000 visitors to the small city of Selma, and a large number to re-enact the final leg of the march ending in Montgomery. The commemoration led to the opportunity for engagement in a

Edmund Pettus Bridge, Selma Alabama 2015.

variety of events, with crowds hearing and seeing activists legends Bob Moses, Diane Nash and talk of the need for continued social and political action.

The ongoing return to the Selma to Montgomery march was no guarantee that the landmarks constituting the historic event would remain. Nothing is permanent except impermanence, and the sites that freshman journeyers look forward to seeing each year could disappear without proactive, decisive action.

Informing Publics about the March through Place

The National Trails System Act, passed in 1968 by Congress, made it possible for a series of historic sites to be preserved together, to tell the comprehensive story of an event or era in time. Federal legislation sponsored by Congressman John Lewis was passed in 1990 amending the National Trails System Act, enabling the National Park Service to conduct the Selma to Montgomery study, with these defining words:

"The route from Selma to Montgomery, Alabama traveled by people in a march dramatizing the need for voting rights legislation, in March 1965, includes Sylvan South Street, Water Avenue, the Edmund Pettus Bridge, and Highway 80. The study under this paragraph shall be prepared in accordance with subsection (b) of this section, except that it shall be completed and submitted to the Congress with recommendations as to the trail's suitability for designation not later than 1 year after the enactment of this paragraph."

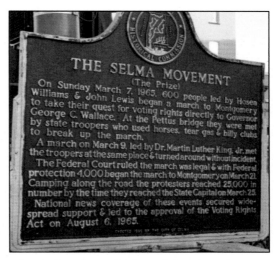

Historical marker at the foot of the Edmund Pettus bridge.

This legislation coincided with a historical marker placed near the bridge.

National Park Service's Barbara Tagger organized materials and public meetings to gather information leading to decisions about sites to be included within the 54 miles stretch between Selma and Montgomery, the location of those sites, and how they could be commemorated. The information gathered would prove the eligibility and feasibility of project. It included oral histories of civil rights participants, conducted in 1990 and 1991.

National Park Service signage for Campsite 3, Selma to Montgomery Trail.

National Park Service signage for Campsite 2, Selma to Montgomery Trail.

The final product conformed to the high expectations of the public and the Secretary of the Interior, and in 1995 Rep. John Lewis introduced a H.R. 1129, a bill amending the National Trails System Act to make Selma to Montgomery the nation's ninth National Park Service trail. The following year, P.L. 104-333, Section 501 of the National Trails System Act established the Selma to Montgomery National Trail, with an award of $1.5 million for its development.

Tagger's work has also contributed to the development of the Martin Luther King Jr. National Park Site and the Harriet Tubman National Monument in Maryland. From Edwin Bearss:

"The lead in undertaking the study that resulted in a finding by the National Park System Advisory Board that the Selma to Montgomery March Trail meets the criteria for designation as a National Historic Trail was undertaken by Lake Lambert and Barbara Tagger, a pair of young and capable historians assigned to the Service's Southeast Regional Office. Contact with key players in the Dallas County Voters League, SNCC and Southern Christian Leadership Council (SCLC), and the community identified by Representative Lewis was established."

Barbara Tagger and Alabama Congresswoman Terri Sewell.

Detail, Edmund Pettus bridge, Selma, Alabama.

Detail, Edmund Pettus bridge, Selma, Alabama.

172

The entire march site is maintained by the National Park Service as a national trail. Individual sites on the trail that have been preserved and placed on the National Register of Historic Places include Brown Chapel A.M.E. Church, where the march began, and the Alabama State Capitol building. Additional commemoratives have been put in place since that time.

Alabama State House, Montgomery, Alabama, 1965. The State House is part of the National Park Service Selma to Montgomery National Trail.

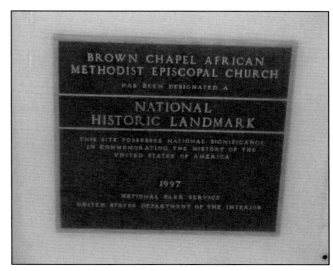

National Historic Landmark plaque for Brown Chapel AME Church. Brown Chapel in a site in the Selma to Montgomery National Trail.

Mural at the head of the Edmund Pettus bridge.

Left of mural at the head of the Edmund Pettus bridge.

Middle of mural at the head of the Edmund Pettus bridge.

Right of mural at the head of the Edmund Pettus bridge.

174

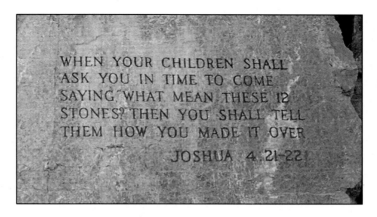

Inscription on stone monument at the head of the Edmund Pettus Bridge, Selma, Alabama.

Monuments at the head of the Edmund Pettus bridge, Selma, Alabama.

Monuments at the head of the Edmund Pettus bridge, Selma, Alabama.

Monuments at the head of the Edmund Pettus bridge, Selma, Alabama.

Monuments at the head of the Edmund Pettus bridge, Selma, Alabama.

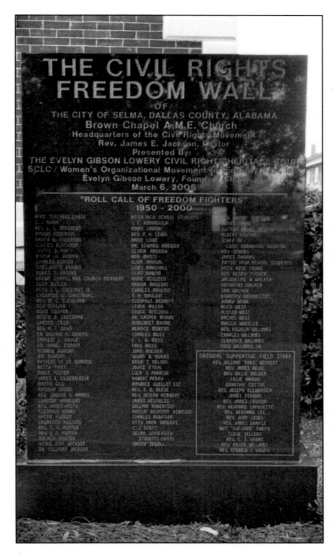

Monument on the grounds of Brown Chapel AME Church, Selma, Alabama.

Viola Liuzzo memorial marker on Highway 80, Selma, Alabama.

Viola Liuzzo memorial marker on Highway 80, Selma, Alabama.

At this writing, Barbara Tagger is Site Manager for the National Park Service Selma to Montgomery National Historic Trail. Tagger has served the National Park Service for more than 30 years as a research historian and historic preservationist, participating in the creation, development, and management of the Selma to Montgomery Trail, but also the Martin Luther King, Jr. National Historic Site; the Tuskegee Airmen National Historic Site and the Tuskegee Institute National Park, where she served as acting superintendent.

In 2007, the Maryland Department of Natural Resources, Maryland Park Service recruited Barbara to act as interim project manager for the Harriet Tubman Underground Railroad State Park Initiative. She was the public face for the state project, assisting with planning and development of interpretive exhibits; oversight of interpretive publications, programming, educational activities, and multimedia programs. Among her honors are the 2013 Harriet Tubman Lifetime Achievement Award presented by the Baltimore African American Tourism Council in Maryland, with the successful establishment of the Harriet Tubman Underground Railroad National Monument in 2013 and the 2002 William C. Everhart award for sustained achievements within the National Park Service. She has taught and continues to inform in many venues, including on C-Span.

Frontiers of Activism in Consecrated Sites

In the introduction, it was argued that a conscious public can generate the support and political will critical not only to save civil rights sites, but also to ensure that the sites promote political engagement and social uplift of those most injured by discriminatory practices. It is argued here that civil rights, human rights and social movement sites, through preservation, through creative inclusion in film and television, through re-enactments and through specific types of onsite activities, CAN and MUST advance the achievement of a just and equitable present.

Throughout this book, numerous sites were selected to illustrate the power of good through preservation. But every one of them pales in comparison to the impact of the preservation and maintenance of Mother Emanuel AME Church, a civil rights legend that has, and is projected to have a great increase in generating common good described above.

Mother Emanuel AME Church in downtown Charleston, South Carolina, previously recognized as the church started by revolutionary Denmark Vesey, burnt to the ground and rebuilt, entered history anew on June 17, 2015. On that day, as most people made preparations to close out their day, a startling news item burst through the media chatter and normalcy of the evening routine. Word of mouth spread an unbelievable story: a 21 year old white male walked into the church to join parishioners at bible study, and then an hour into the program, gunned down nine church members. Only three survived the deadly shooting. One of those murder victims was a South Carolina State Senator, Rev. Clementa Pinckney, who had been a champion for legislation that would bring justice and equity to the suffering in his district, as well as the pastor of Mother Emanuel.

Built in 1891, the church still retains its original altar, communion rail and light fixtures. It survived an 1872 earthquake to stand as the oldest African Methodist Episcopal church in the South.

Its congregation has its roots in a group of free blacks and slaves who organized in 1791. Its first significant 'earthquake' was the result of one of its founders, Denmark Vesey, a slave from the Virgin Islands who had purchased his freedom and organized a slave rebellion in December 1821, in order to obtain freedom for others. The plot was discovered, causing a panic throughout the South, and Vesey and 35 others were executed. Mother Emanuel was investigated in 1822 in relation to the rebellion, and eventually burned to the ground. The church was rebuilt but closed when all-black churches were outlawed in South Carolina in 1834, leaving the congregation to meet in secret until the end of the Civil War in 1865, and the name Emanuel chosen.

One hundred and fifty years after the rebirth of Emanuel, the end of the Civil War and the freedom of slaves observed by Juneteenth, the horrific acts that struck at the heart of this church also struck the soul of the nation. While the accused murderer was quickly caught and brought to court, where he confessed his crimes, the particulars of the attack, combined with the historic status of the site, struck a nerve with the nation and world, resulting in an outpouring of good and a stimulus toward social, political and economic change.

Mother Emanuel was not the subject of total restoration and major preservation in the same manner as the other sites. Though it is not individually listed in the National Register of Historic Places, Mother Emanuel is a contributing property to the Charleston Old Historic District, which is listed, and is included in a National Park Service guide to Religious sites in Charleston, created in collaboration with the City of Charleston. But the years of commitment to this land, coupled with the events that took place, led to social events that could be the early rumblings of seismic changes in state and national history.

The first is an increased attention to racism, the expression of need to understand the history of slavery, civil rights and racism in the United States. This need was addressed by *#CharlestonSyllabus*, a list of readings about race violence in America and the history of race relations in South Carolina, compiled by Dr. Chad Williams, Chair of Brandeis University's Afro-American Studies Department. This online listing echoed an earlier creation of *#Fergusonsyllabus*, created by Georgetown University professor Marcia Chatelein.   In addition to receiving more historical information and context, communities felt the need to increase understanding through public dialogue and discussion about race. More than 1,000 members joined the Courage Campaign, a South Carolina dialogue effort. Many more thousands participated in demonstrations of Unity at festivals, special events, and bridge crossings. Joseph Riley, Mayor of Charleston, also indicated that before the end of his final term, he would finish the fundraising needed to complete the International African American Museum, which at the time needed $75 million additional dollars. The Museum would also support ongoing conversations as well as feature an exhibit on the Charleston Nine and Mother Emanuel.

The additional resources required in this tragedy were also an outgrowth of efforts to make social change. Palmetto Project, a Charleston based statewide nonprofit organization which had previously worked with Senator Pinckney and with Mother Emanuel Church, launched the Reverend Pinckney Fund to continue his social and political efforts. The City of Charleston set up a Mother Emanuel Fund to support the families of the Charleston Nine. The amount they raised included a $3 million dollar gift to pay for the education of the children.

Mother Emanuel itself, and the role it played in civil rights history, was a story that spread around the world. The individuals who lost their lives became the Charleston Nine, and they, as well as the church building, were memorialized through song, art, and other symbolic imagery. Their story was connected to others who sacrificed for civil rights, such as the Friendship Nine of Rock Hill. Other connections became abundantly clear; on instance is that two of those killed were alumni of Allen University in Columbia. One of those alumni, Senator Clementa Pinckney, lay in state on the third floor of the South Carolina State House, under the rotunda, and was funeralized by South Carolina House member Reverend Joseph H. Neal, South Carolina Senator Gerald Malloy and Senior AME Bishop John Richard Bryant, with the eulogy offered by President Barack Obama. The funeral was televised nationally, and attended by First Lady Michelle Obama and Vice President Joe Biden and Second Lady Dr. Jill Biden; also by Governor Nikki Haley and former Secretary of State Hillary Clinton. A bipartisan Congressional delegation, led by House Speaker John Boehner and Majority Leader Mitch McConnell, and including Rep. John Lewis, House Majority Whip Steve Scalise, South Carolina Congressman James E. Clyburn, the highest ranking African American in Congress, and House Minority Whip Steny Hoyer. Also in attendance were activists Rev. Jesse Jackson and the Rev. Al Sharpton. These individuals would return to South Carolina, to watch the Confederate flag debate and its ultimate removal, and to a 2016 Faith and Politics pilgrimage to the state.

Reporters are briefed for the accused's first Charleston Court appearance since the slayings.

Commemorative banner on building next to Mother Emanuel AME Church, Charleston July 2015.

Historian Jack Bass in attendance at the
Pinckney funeral.

Funeral service for Senator Clementa Pinckney in Charleston.

The next element of change, the fight to remove the Confederate flag from the South Carolina State House grounds, which began in the 1980s with efforts led by South Carolina Senator Kay Patterson to remove the flag from the top of the Capitol dome, gained national traction with the Charleston Nine murders. On June 25th, the day before the funeral for Senator Pinckney, the Congressional Black Caucus

Take Down the Flag Rally, South Carolina State House grounds.

submitted a resolution honoring the 'Emanuel 9', and calling for the removal of the flag from the State House grounds. Charleston elected officials also took up the call, and soon corporations like Walmart, NASCAR, and Amazon took positions against the flag.

Tom Hall, a South Carolina native, organized a rally and a Unity Festival to bring down the flag, and the nation watched as South Carolina's Governor, Nikki Haley, called legislators back into session to address removal of the flag. Once the body voted to approve debate on the flag removal, C-span, CNN and other national press followed the debates closely. The Senate passed a bill to remove the flag from the Grounds, followed by emotionally charged debate by the South Carolina House. With the bill passed by both bodies of the South Carolina legislature, the bill was signed into a law by the Governor in a public ceremony, at which the widow of Senator Pinckney was present. Thousands witnessed, and viewers across the country watched as the Confederate flag was removed and handed off to the Director of the Confederate Museum. The removal was complete, with the pole and the concrete base taken up as well.

Take Down the Flag rally participants hold up original signs and images of Mother Emanuel AME Church.

Rep. James Emerson Smith, Jr., South Carolina House, after his speech at the Take Down the Flag rally.

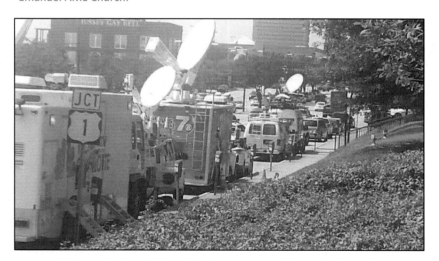

Press out in force for the signing of the law to remove the Confederate flag from the South Carolina State House grounds.

Nelson Rivers III, National Action Network, and attorney Tom Turnipseed present for the signing.

Rev. Jesse Jackson, who was on hand for Legislative deliberations on the flag, greets Emanuel Nine family members at the signing.

Governor Nikki Haley, flanked by former Governors, legislators and supporters, makes remarks before signing the bill.

The desk where the law removing the Confederate flag from the State House grounds was signed, as seen through a television camera lens.

Removal of the Confederate Flag: Symbol or Substance?

We cannot deny the power that comes from the existence of these buildings. Our built environment tells us what is important and what is not. Those buildings that remain untouched over time let us know what a community has agreed to as worthy of the resources required to maintain them. From the State Houses that grace every capital city, to church buildings, statues and memorials, street signs and historic districts, the sense of what is important is

Former Governor David Beasley, whose position on the Confederate flag contributed to his 1998 re-election defeat, reflects with a reporter.

everywhere. This idea is what led over 50,000 citizens of South Carolina and other states to rally to bring the Confederate Flag down from its location atop the State House. It is what leads some buildings to be bulldozed and others protected.

Historian Marcia G. Synnott supported an alternative in her 2007 case study of the South Carolina State House and Grounds. Her preference, rather than "toppling" statues, is to revise their interpretation. First through official websites, then through plaques or markers placed near the monument that carry revised interpretation that will place the subject's words or actions into context. Finally, the revision should be included in assigned textbooks in South Carolina history courses. Synott asserts that it is the task of historians and scholars to provide this context and interpretation. Others support a focus on changes to economic, political and social policy that will alleviate poverty, racism, and inequity, rather than a focus on symbols such as flags and monuments.

This 'toppling', or removal of the Confederate flag, can be compared to the impacts of the removal of the Berlin Wall. In Ronald Reagan's famous

Observers in a nearby office building watch the final lowering of the Confederate flag from the State House grounds.

remarks at the Brandenburg Gate in 1987, he spoke of Mr. Gorbachev and 'new policies of reform and openness', as signs that the then Soviets were 'coming to understand the importance of freedom'. Reagan further asked, "Are these the beginnings of profound changes in the Soviet state? Or are they token gestures, intended to raise false hopes in the West, or to strengthen the Soviet system without changing it?" He went on, in his famous quote, to call for 'the one sign the Soviets can make that would be unmistakable, that would advance dramatically the cause of peace and freedom' Reagan called upon Gorbachev, "If you seek peace, if you seek prosperity for the Soviet Union and Eastern Europe, come here to this gate! Mr. Gorbachev, open this gate! Mr. Gorbachev, tear down this wall!" Reagan stated that the hour of his demand represented a moment of hope for the embrace of a new set of values, in a move that combined symbolism and policy.

Removal of the wall, and the re-unification of East and West Germany, proved indeed to be a combination of symbol and substance. Germany is now one of the most economically secure nation-states in the world, with adequate resources to provide public health care, and other social service supports. Continued separation, fragmentation and polarization within a nation-state have desperate implications both within and between many nations. Rwanda is just one example:

> *"In April of 1994 during the 100 terrifying days of the Rwandan genocide, Tutsi civilians took refuge at the Nyamata Church in Bugesera, hoping to escape the atrocities of the killings around them. The church was supposed to be a safe haven as no one believed anyone would kill people on holy ground. Eventually the Hutu militia broke down the gates and slaughtered over 10,000 innocent people with machetes, grenades and rifles.*
>
> *I walked through the mass gravesite that holds the bones, skulls and clothing of many of the victims of this heinous act. I felt surrounded by death and sadness and I can't help but think of my own struggling culture. But then my view expands to all people all over the world and all of the suffering we inflict on ourselves when we are capable of such empathy, love and compassion. I have to believe that we can overcome such hatred and evil. I absolutely have to believe we are all capable of so much more."*
>
> *~Rand Courtney, filmmaker*

Ntarama Church, Bugesera Region, Kigali, Rwanda.

Although the Confederate flag and its meaning remain contentious issues, its removal from the dome of the State House and later from its place near the Confederate Monument on the State House grounds was a form of toppling. Sufficient public sentiment about its negative meaning, and the circumstances of its placement on government property made it clear that removal, not

Ntarama Church, Bugesera Region, Kigali, Rwanda.

reinterpretation, was the order and imperative of the day. The murders of the Charleston Nine brought many more around the country to reach this conclusion.

Removal of the flag itself, a decision that would come as the result of public sentiment, moral courage and legislative action, as great a message of triumph as that would be, would be but a beginning. Just as more solvent countries pledge to help emerging democracies make the transition, our entire community must continue to eliminate all the false narratives that embrace hatred rather than unity. How much stronger, then, is a community that preserves its sites not just as symbols and locations for historical memory, but also as working places for making positive social change and eliminating racism, sexism and so many other social evils? What do we risk if we do not make these changes?

Frontiers of Social Change in Sacred Space

With a renewed sense of the critical value of these sacred sites and all that they inspire, this section delves into the limits and promise of civil rights sacred spaces. Despite the passion that many have for these spaces and buildings, and the willingness to expend years to make them permanent fixtures in our communities, there are some who express different social priorities, especially given the competition for limited funds. If these sites are valued, it is imperative to understand the arguments against them, and to make a persuasive case to the public that investing resources in these sites is a justifiable position, not merely from a tourism, economic development or preservationist point of view, but also from the standpoint of advancing public good, and justice from civil and human rights perspectives.

A ready example of this conflict can be found in efforts in Mississippi to save these spaces. During early efforts by Mississippi Governor Haley Barbour to develop and promote civil rights tourism, long-time activists C.T. Vivian and Diane Nash published an open letter questioning the development of civil rights tourism and spaces, asking who benefits. Nash argued that the beneficiaries were people outside the communities of African Americans who moved the civil rights struggle forward, and communities that remain in financial distress. Nash has a strong moral position from which to argue: she is one of the founding members of the Student Nonviolent Coordinating Committee (SNCC), leaving academics at Fisk behind to focus on planning and carrying out strategies that would challenge and end the racism she experienced in Tennessee. She emerged as one of the leaders of SNCC, with her quiet refusal to turn back even in the face of dangerous and angry individuals who were willing to fight and kill to maintain a system of segregation in southern communities.

From Nash's point of view, the work in saving these sites does not produce a better income and a better quality of life for black communities that need jobs and opportunity. What's more, the revenue from these sites that are critical spaces born of the blood and sacrifice of black people is syphoned off to other communities. What does not uplift in a tangible way is not acceptable to Nash.

Along the same lines is the decades-long protest of Jacqueline Smith in Memphis, who believes that the funding spent on the Lorraine Motel and the National Civil Rights Museum should have been used to help the poor around the community through direct services. Her point of view suggests that civil rights hallowed ground could and should do more to promote the political and economic agenda of civil rights struggle, not just the legacy. Her passion for this cause could be clearly seen as equal to the passion of those who have worked for a decade or more to make the sites available to everyone. Smith's view is that the decision to save and transform the place where Dr. King's life ended was actually an injustice, where poor people who need financial support were on the losing end.

Are communities better off because civil rights battlegrounds have been saved? Does 'never forget' lead to action? Do African American communities benefit when civil rights tourism, museums, re-enactments or films are created? Should they? If so, in what form should that benefit come? Would the money be better spent on social, economic uplift and political programs, as some activists say?

A strong case can be made that communities are indeed better off when their civil rights landscapes are preserved for current and future generations. In order for these sacred sites to offer the maximum social and political returns for their communities, those communities must make these commitments a priority:

- *Validating sites by providing a financial and organizational structure that promotes longevity, stability, sustainability and independent action.*

Many civil and human rights sites struggle to become established, and struggle to remain solvent. They need broad support from a cross section of communities to advocate for them, to ensure a regular stream of public and private funding, to that they have long term stability. It is also important to recognize limits in what can be done politically because sites are often connected with

Hillary's visit to the Harriet Tubman house in Auburn, NY as part of Saving America's Treasures on 7/15/98.

organizations that have a non-profit charitable organizations status, restricting their ability to lobby for policy or advocate for legislation that would creation social change. In order to avoid this restriction, organizations that manage and operate civil and human rights sites should explore effective affiliation with organizations internally structured to allow political action and advocacy.

Those sites that are locally recognized as historic sites, or have attained National Register of Historic Places status, are eligible for funding to assist with restoration costs. Often there is limited funding available through this path, and much competition for those funds. Save America's Treasures, a federal program championed by Hillary Clinton during her tenure as First Lady, provided much needed funding support to the following civil and human rights historic sites:

- ❖ *Sixteenth Street Baptist Church, Birmingham, AL;*
- ❖ *King Memorial Baptist Church, Montgomery, AL;*
- ❖ *National Voting Rights Museum, Selma, AL;*
- ❖ *Rosa Parks Museum, Troy State University, Montgomery, AL;*
- ❖ *Central High School National Historic Site, Little Rock, AR;*
- ❖ *Harriet Beecher Stowe House, Hartford CT;*
- ❖ *Mary Church Terrell House, Washington DC;*
- ❖ *Morehouse College MLK papers, Atlanta GA;*
- ❖ *Ebenezer Baptist Church, MLK Jr., Atlanta, GA;*
- ❖ *Rosa Parks Bus, Dearborn, MI;*
- ❖ *Medgar Evers Site, Jackson, MS;*
- ❖ *Tougaloo Civil Rights Collection, Tougaloo, MS;*
- ❖ *Harriet Tubman Historic Sites, Auburn NY;*

- ❖ *F.W. Woolworth Building in Greensboro NC;*

- ❖ *Modjeska Simkins House, Columbia, SC;*

- ❖ *Benjamin E. Mayes Birthplace, Greenwood, SC.*

Communities must support programs that make saving civil and human right sites possible, while making sure that the funding mechanism does not constrain political thought and advocacy at the sites.

- o *Stressing strategies and goals of the movement, especially community organizing and extended political discussion, argumentation and persuasion carried out by its 'non-elite' grass roots members.*

The work of the sites must include community organization, with opportunities for direct action, lobbying, advocating and developing political agendas. Time and energy must also be devoted to critical thinking and reflection, to debate and analysis, to re-examination to roles, goals and strategies in the work of advancing movements. This work is often left by the wayside in the effort to generate 'wins' on the political agenda column. Without it, true evolution and revolution will not happen, particularly at the grass roots level, where emphasis placed on dialogue, thought, reflection and analysis reap critical benefits. In the process of doing this, these sacred sites will be a part of revitalizing of the public sphere: locally based gathering places that create opportunities for extended thought and discussion, fostering the development of political voices that share a common vision.

o *Moving beyond discussion of rights, justice, equality and freedom concepts to facilitation of experiences that constitute political action toward fulfilling those concepts.*

Observances of Martin Luther King Jr. Day at Edmund Pettus Bridge, 2015.

In addition to discussions on historical action and concepts of justice, the sacred spaces have an obligation to provide opportunities to do more than commemorate and facilitate understanding of the past. Organizations like the International Sites of Conscience and the American Association of Museums offer historical sites the tools to apply the stories of their unique histories in such a way as to increase the relationship between museum activity and interpretive materials and modern day concerns. But communities must demand that sacred spaces of justice embrace their dual roles of education of historical past and their contribution to creating a just reality. This reconstruction of the mission of these sites, often dictated by boards and councils, will not happen without strong community commitment, demand for change, and support for required funding.

Observances of Martin Luther King Jr. Day at Edmund Pettus Bridge, 2015.

o *Providing funding and support for social change projects; lobbying and advocating for policies that promote social change, and against those which stifle change or have a disproportionate negative impact on black and brown communities.*

Sacred sites should structure themselves, or ally themselves with structures that foster the growth and strength of new movements and organizations. They should seek to provide funding support for new projects that will make change happen in their communities. They should seek to maximize their ability to generate funds through tourism and other sources that can be redistributed into new projects that help make poor communities stronger and more capable of growth.

Take Down the Flag Rally participant holds up his Voter Registration Card.

Public Housing near Brown Chapel AME Church in Selma, Alabama.

○ *Making a stronger connection between sacred spaces as places that connect history with the ongoing work of providing social and restorative justice.*

Despite the broad use of social media platforms by leaders of social movements like Black Lives Matter, the young are not immune from the strong connection that historical places offer. Charlene A. Carruthers, a leader of Black Youth 100 and activist in the Black Lives Matter movement, has visited other countries and stood at the sites where revolution has taken place. "Haiti's history isn't just fascinating to me as a junior historian, it's essential to me as an organizer committed to Black liberation." Carruthers said in a tweet on December 24, 2015.

Recognition of the strength that these sacred sites offer means that we should respond to the call to support civil and human rights sites, and incorporate them as an integral part of the struggle. This should be done so that every neighborhood and community of color in the area feels not just welcome, but ownership. All sacred spaces should provide such supports as a base of operation for strategic planning events, and free use of meeting space by all organizations focused on ending racism, sexism, income equality, homelessness, support for efforts by Native Americans, fair housing, and other social ills. These organizations must reciprocate by making sure they support the site and its financial needs in remaining a sustainable haven for their efforts.

The opportunity is there, to reach out to impoverished communities that are still in need of a vision and a way forward, a set of values that can uplift, and a strategy that will allow new generations of walkers to step in the footsteps of their forbearers. Many of these civil and human rights sites remain in the heart of just those communities, where the proper strategies, imbued with the winds of freedom and the songs of victory echoing from days past, can entice, embolden and invite new generations from many futures to join the work.

Creating internal structures within organizations that operate civil and human rights sites must also support both electoral and movement politics. Black Lives Matter and Occupy Wall Street provide our best example of movement politics, which are social movements created by groups of people working together, based on their ideologies, or what they believe about the social, economic and political structure of their communities. On the electoral politics side is those who support voter registration, groom and help candidates run successfully for office, and support political responses to social problems.

Civil and Human Rights historical sites with the power to be a unifying force for various organizations in social movements, to lobby for specific bills and laws, to educate about the impact of laws is a crucial next step for these sites. Those who can provide assistance for legislators who do not have large staffs, can provide independent policy experts who can publicize legislation, conduct issue advocacy campaigns that unify those in social movements, and testify on behalf of bills is the true next frontier for civil and human rights historical sites. It is up to private citizens, working collectively, to make that potential a reality.

Photography Credits

Layout: Justin M. Long

Cover design: 18th Street Design, LLC

Bibliography

Aba-Mecha, Barbara Woods. *Black Woman Activist in Twentieth Century South Carolina: Modjeska Monteith Simkins.* Dissertation. Emory University, 1978.

Bailey, D'Army. The Education of a Black Radical: A Southern Civil Rights Activist's Journey 1959-1964. Baton Rouge: Louisiana State University Press, 2009, pp. 54,68,138,186,206-8, 221.

Bailey, D'Army. Mine Eyes Have Seen: Dr. Martin Luther King Jr.'s Final Journey. Memphis: Towery Publishing, Inc., 1993.

Bearss, Edwin. *Oral History: Deliering a Powerful Interpretive Message.* 1993 No. 10 supplement, Cultural Resource Management, A publication of the National Park Service. US Department of the Interior. http://www.msnbc.com/msnbc/michael-brown-memorial-ferguson-rebuilt

Blessey, Mary. Minnie Watson interview, Jackson Free Press. July 20, 2011.

Botsch, Carol. *African Americans in the Palmetto State.* South Carolina Department of Education. 1994.

Campbell, Yolanda Denise. Outsiders within: A framing analysis of eight Black and White U.S. newspapers' coverage of the Civil Rights Movement, 1954—1964. The University of Southern Mississippi, ProQuest, UMI Dissertations Publishing, 2011.

Carson, Clayborne. "Civil Rights Reform and the Black Freedom Struggle," in Charles W. Eagles (ed.), The Civil Rights Movement in America. (Jackson: University of Mississippi Press, 1986), 19-37.

Classen, Steven. *Watching Jim Crow: The Struggles over Mississippi TV, 1955-1969.* Durham and London: Duke University Press, 2004.

Conlon, S.F. 'A Hospital Built By Them, For Them. The Good Samaritan Waverly Hospital Building Fund Campaign and the Evolution of Black Healthcare Traditions in Columbia. Dissertation. University of South Carolina 2012.

Davis, Rebecca Miller. Reporting race and resistance in Dixie: The white Mississippi press and civil rights, 1944—1964. University of South Carolina, ProQuest, UMI Dissertations Publishing, 2011.

Dufresne, Marcel. Exposing the Secrets of Mississippi Racism: To the Dismay of Some, the Clarion-Ledger is Mining the Bitter Past: the Medgar Evers Murder, State Spies and Its Own Unsavory Record. Washington Journalism Review. October 1991, Vol. 13, Issue 8, p36-40.

Eskew, Glenn T. 'Memorializing the Movement: The Struggle to Build Civil Rights Museums in the South",

Evers and Peters, For Us, the Living, 269.

Fairclough, Adam. "State of the Art: Historians and the Civil Rights Movement Journal of American Studies (1990), 24: 387-398 Cambridge University Press 1990.

Farley, Reynolds. 'The Kerner Commission Report Plus Four Decades: What Has Changed, What Has Not". Population Studies Center Research Report 08-656. Ann Arbor, MI: 2008.

Gergel, Belinda and Richard. 'In Pursuit of the Tree of Life: A History of the Early Jews of Columbia, South Carolina, and the Tree of Life Congregation. Columbia, SC: Tree of Life Congregation, 1996.

Haley, Alex. Autobiography of Malcolm X.

Hilmes, Michele. Only Connect: A Cultural History of Broadcasting in the United States. Cengage Learning, 2010.

Hine, Darlene Clark. "Black Victory: The Rise and Fall of the White Primary in Texas". Millwood, NY: K.T.O. Press, 1979.

Hoerl, Kristen. Mississippi's Social Transformation in Public Memories of the Trial Against Byron de la Beckwith for the Murder of Medgar Evers. Western Journal of Communication. Jan-Mar2008, Vol. 72 Issue 1, p62-82. 21p.

Hoffman, Erwin D. 'The Genesis of the Modern Movement for Equal Rights in South Carolina, 1930-1939.' In *The Negro in Depression and War: Prelude to Revolution, 1930-1945*. Bernard Sternsher, ed. Quadrangle Books, Chicago IL. 1969.

Horowitz, Robert B. Broadcast Reform Revisited: Reverend Everett C Parker and the "Standing" Case. (Office of Communication of the United Church of Christ v. Federal Communications Commission). The Communication Review. Vol. 2, No. 3 (1997).

Jansen, Holly. *From Selma to Montgomery: Remembering Alabama's Civil Rights Movement Through Museums.* University of Florida Masters' Thesis, 2012.

Johnson, Thomas L. 'Black & white world of Richard Roberts.' The State Magazine, Columbia, SC. January 6, 1985.

Lau, Peter. 'Mr. NAACP: Levi G. Byrd and the Remaking of the NAACP in state and nation: 1917-1960. Winfred B. Moore Jr. and Orville Vernon Burton, eds. *Toward the meeting of the Waters: Currents in the Civil Rights movement of South Carolina during the twentieth century.* USC Press 2008.

Marable, Manning. Living Black History: How Reimagining the African-American Past Can Remake America's Racial Future. Cambridge: Basic Civitas Books, 2006.

Marsh, Charles. 'God's Long Summer: Stories of Faith and Civil Rights".1997 Princeton University Press, New Jersey.

Massey, Douglas and Nancy A. Denton, *American Apartheid: Segregation and the Making of the Underclass.* Harvard University Press, 1993.

Marable, Manning and Leith Mullings, eds. *Let Nobody Turn Us Around, Voices of Resistance, Reform and Renewal: An African American Anthology*. Maryland, Rowman and Littlefield, 2000.

Mills, Kay. *Changing Channels: The Civil Rights Case that Transformed Television.* Jackson: University Press of Mississippi, 2004.

Minow, Newton N. and Craig L. May. *Inside the Presidential Debates: Their Improbable Past and Promising Future.* University of Chicago Press, 2008.

Moore, Winifred B., Kyle S. Smith and David White, eds. *Warm Ashes: Issues in Southern History at the Dawn of the 21st Century*

Moore, Winifred B., Jr. and Orville Vernon Burton, eds. *Toward the meeting of the Waters: Currents in the Civil Rights movement of South Carolina during the twentieth century.* University of South Carolina Press, 2008.

Myrdal, Gunnar, Richard Sterner, and Arnold Rose. *An American Dilemma.* New York: Harper and Brothers, 1944.

Powell, Tamara. "Willie Lee Buffington and Faith Cabin Libraries", in *Grappling with Diversity: Readings on Civil Rights Pedagogy and Critical Multiculturalism,* Susan Schramm-Pate, Rhonda Baynes Jeffries, ed. SUNY Press, 2008.

Ricchiardi, Sherry. "Out of the Past." *American Journalism Review* 27, no. 2, 2005.

Roberts, Gene and Hank Klibanoff. *The Race Beat: The Press, The Civil Rights Struggle, and the Awakening of a Nation.* New York: Random House, 2006.

Roefs, Wim. 'The Impact of 1940s Civil Rights Activism on the State's 1960s Civil Rights Scene: A Hypothesis and Historiographical Discussion', found in: Moore, Winifred B., Jr. and Orville Vernon Burton, eds. *Toward the meeting of the Waters: Currents in the Civil Rights movement of South Carolina during the twentieth century.* USC Press 2008.

Rolph, Stephanie Renee. "In unity there is strength": The "Clarion-Ledger's coverage of the Medgar Evers murder. Mississippi State University, ProQuest. UMI Dissertations Publishing, 2004.

Rose, Vivien Ellen. "Men Make no mention of Her Heroism": Natural and Cultural Resources and Women's Past. Organization of American Historians Magazine of History. 12 (Fall 1997).

Rowe, Maggie and Ken Taylor, eds. 'New Cultural Landscapes'. Routledge 2014.

Sales, William W. From Civil Rights to Black Liberation: Malcolm X and the Organization of African Unity. South End Press, 1994.

Salter, Jr., John R. Jackson, Mississippi: An American Chronicle of Struggle and Schism (Hicksville: Exposition Press, 1979).

South by Southeast. 'Roberts Photographs Are Published'. University of South Carolina, Columbia, 1984.

Sponhour, Michael. *Parks brings 'living history.* The State Newspaper. July 28, 1996.

Tagger, Barbara. *Interpreting African American Women's History Through Historic Landscapes, Structures and Sites.* Organization of American Historians. 12, 1, Fall 1997.

Tisdale, John R. "Medgar Evers (1925-1963) and the Mississippi Press." Ph.D. diss. University of North Texas, 1996.

Torres, Sasha. Black. White. and in Color: Television and Black Civil Rights. Princeton and Oxford: Princeton University Press, 2003.

Williams, Julian. "The Truth Shall Make You Free." *Journalism History* 32, no. 2: 106-113, 2006.

Williams, Michael Vinson. Medgar Evers : Mississippi Martyr. Fayetteville, AR, USA: The University of Arkansas Press, 2011.

Newspaper articles

'Additional comments: Rev. John Jacob Starks, D.D. in 'Seneca Institute/Seneca Junior College'. Historical Marker Database. Published February 2010. http://www.hmdb.org/marker.asp?marker=27333

'Along the NAACP Battlefront: Sit-ins in South Carolina' The Crisis magazine, April 1961.

At Spike Lee's Gallery: Commentary, Expressions of Art. http://blackandbrownnews.com/galleries/photos/spike-lees-joint-social-commentary-expression-art/

Carney, Jordain. "Southern Cities to Celebrate Civil Rights 50th Anniversary". Scripps Howard Foundation Wire, Spring 2012.

'College and School News', The Crisis, August-Sept. 1961.

"Ezel Ford autopsy." Los Angeles Times. December 29, 2014. http://www.latimes.com/local/lanow/la-me-ln-ezell-ford-autopsy-20141229-story.html#page=1

Ferguson Civil Rights March Reaches Halfway point. Lynne Roberts. Ww.jrn.com/khs/news/ferguson-civil-rights-march-reaches-halfway-point-284687971.html

James Earl Chaney Foundation. Website. http://jecf.org/freedomsummer/freedomsummer2004/index.html

"Jim's Blog", Jim Somerville, Pastor, Richmond's First Baptist Church. https://jimsomerville.wordpress.com/2009/01/19/here-cometh-the-dreamer/

'Judge Proud of Role in Exonerating Friendship Nine in Rock Hill', February 1, 2015, David Perlmutt, Charlotte Observer. http://www.charlotteobserver.com/news/local/article9503723.html

'Landmarks Omission'. Kemba Johnson. City Limits. September 1, 1998.

'*Medgar Evers Home Donated to Tougaloo (MS) College*. Jet magazine, April 5, 1993.

Medgar Evers Home Reopening After Preservation.
http://www.jacksonfreepress.com/news/2013/jun/11/medgar-evers-home-reopening-after-preservation/

Paul Hampel, St. Louis Dispatch, September 24, 2014.
http://www.stltoday.com/news/local/metro/ferguson-residents-rebuild-michael-brown-memorial-after-fire/article_e8e2f039-4fd0-5c0a-ae04-474f4b1df194.html

'Protestors Blast Plan to Raze Audubon', Jeffrey Kantrowitz, Columbia Daily Spectator, Volume CXIV, No. 113, April 6, 1990.

The Brawley-Starks Center, Morris College, Morris College. Website.
http://www.morris.edu/brawley-starks-academic-success-center

The Washington Post. http://newseum.org/programs/2013/0605-special-program/the-legacy-of-civil-rights-leader-medgar-evers.html

USA Today. http://www.usatoday.com/story/news/2013/06/02/medgar-evers-arts/2378249/&ct=ga&cad=CAcQARgBIAAoATAAOABAz7GrjQVIAVAAWABiBWVuLVVT&cd=9mO59RBKHa8&usg=AFQjCNFoajPYCwg6VqsSwsFyjIXARn8Veg

"What the Branches Are Doing", The Crisis magazine, October 1960.

Primary Sources

Aaron Henry interview by T.H. Baker, September 12, 1970. Lyndon B. Johnson Library, Austin TX. http://www.lbjlib.utexas.edu/johnson/archives.hom/oralhistory.hom/Henry-A/Henry01.PDF

Aaron Henry, speaking in "On Television: Public Trust or Private Property? A documentary by Films Incorporated, New Brunswick, NJ 1989.

Martti Ahtisaari speech at the J. William Fulbright Prize for International Understanding. Washington, DC. December 1, 2000.

Allen C. Thompson speech, 1-5, Medgar Wiley Evers Collection, Tougaloo College Archives Lillian P. Benbow Room of Special Collections, Tougaloo, Mississippi.

Allen C. Thompson speech, 1-5, Tougaloo College Archives, Lillian Bowman Room, Medgar Wiley Evers collection.

Benedict College Nomination form, National Register of Historic Places. http://www.nationalregister.sc.gov/richland/S10817740096/pages/S1081774009605.htm

Byrd interview, minutes 'State meeting Nov. 10 1939 in Cheraw minutes book. Official program of the First Annual Conference of the South Carolina Conference of Branches, NAACP. Columbia May 17, 1940.

Columbia University and the City of New York 250th Anniversary timeline. http://c250.columbia.edu/c250_events/symposia/history_newyork_timeline.html

H.R. 3834. (101st) Selma to Montgomery National Trail Study Act of 1989. Public Law 101-321.

"In Memory of Senator Isadore Lourie", US Senator Ernest Hollings, Congressional Record – Senate, May 21, 2003.

Investigation of the Assassination of Martin Luther King, Jr. Monday, August 14, 1978. House of
    Representatives Select Committee on Assassinations, Washington DC.
    http://www.usdoj.gov/crt/crim/mlk/part1.htm
Matthew J. Bruccoli letter to the Roberts family. October 10, 1983.

Medgar Evers, letter to the Chairman of the Federal Communications Commission, in Papers of the
    NAACP, Part 20, reel 14 of 15.

Medgar Evers, letter to the Chairman of the Federal Communications Commission, in Papers of the
    NAACP, Part 20, reel 14 of 15 and Letter to Medgar Evers denying Evers' request from Secretary
    Mary Jane Morris, in Papers of the NAACP, Part 20; Medgar Evers letter to Dave Garroway.

Medgar Evers to the Chairman of the Federal Communication Commission, October 17, 1957, Papers of
    the NAACP: Part 20, Group III, Box A-114, microfilm reel 14.

Medgar Evers to the FCC Chairman, October 17, 1957, Docket 16663. Vol 3, FCC files.

Medgar Evers to the Chairman of the FCC, October 17, 1957, and Mary Jane Morris to Medgar Evers
    denying his request, November 19, 1957, Papers of the NAACP: Part 20, Group III, Box A-114,
    microfilm reel 14, and Medgar Evers to Dave Garroway, February 4, 1958, ibid.

Mississippi Department of Archives and History Historical Resources Inventory.

Modjeska Simkins House National Register of Historic Places application. Online:
    http://www.nationalregister.sc.gov/richland/S10817740102/S10817740102.pdf

"NAACP Says Allen Seeking 'Yes-Men,'" Jackson Daily News, May 16, 1963, 16A.

National Association for the Advancement of Colored People. Papers of the NAACP: Part 20, White
    Resistance and Reprisals, 1956-1965. Edited by John H. Bracy, Jr. and August Meier. Bethesda,
    Maryland: University Publications of America, 1995. Microfilm.

National Trust for Historic Preservation, SAVE AMERICA'S TREASURES AWARDS 1999-2010 by State.
http://www.pcah.gov/sites/default/files/SAT%20Awards%201999-2010%20Table_2.pdf

Office of Communications of the United Church of Christ v. Federal Communications Commission, 59
F2d 994 (D.C. Circuit). March 25, 1966.

Press release on "A True Likeness: The Black South of Richard Samuel Roberts, 1920-1936." Bruccoli
Clark, Inc., Columbia, South Carolina, 1986.

Press release on "A True Likeness: The Black South of Richard Samuel Roberts, 1920-1936." C. S.
Pitcher, Publisher, Algonquin Books of Chapel Hill, North Carolina, 1986.

Public Meetings, Draft of Master Plan, Selma to Montgomery Trail. July 10-23, 1997.
http://www.selmafriendsvrt.org/wp-content/uploads/Public-Meeting-Reports-Comments-on-
Draft-Master-Plan.pdf

Report of the National Advisory Commission on Civil Disorders (New York: bantam Books, 1968.

Second Year Report for the President. National Church Arson Task Force: United States Department of
the Treasury, United States Department of Justice, Bureau of Alcohol, Tobacco and Firearms,
Federal Bureau of Investigation. Washington, D.C., October 1998.

The Starks Center, Benedict College Nomination form, National Register of Historic Places.

'The Honorable Hyman S. Rubin: A Concurrent Resolution" S. 1077, a Resolution of the South Carolina
General Assembly, 116th Session, 2005-2006. http://www.schouse.gov/sess116_2005-
2006/bills/1077.htm

Thirtieth Annual Everett C. Parker Ethics in Telecommunications Lecture Rev. Jesse L. Jackson, Sr.,
delivered September 25, 2012.
https://org2.salsalabs.com/o/6587/images/Rev.%20Jesse%20Jackson-
2012%20Parker%20Lecture%20Prepared%20Text.pdf

"Telephone Call from Mr. Current," May 17, 1963, Papers of the NAACP: Part 20, Group III, Box A-232, microfilm reel 2. 23. Medgar Evers, "Remarks of Mr. Medgar Evers, Field Secretary." May 20, 1963, NAACP Papers, LOC, Group III, Box A90, Folder 12, 1.

Window Dressing on the Set: Women and Minorities in Television. 1977. A report of the United States Commission on Civil Rights, Washington, DC.

Index

Reading List

Selma to Montgomery March

David Garrow. *Protest at Selma: Martin Luther King Jr. and the Voting Rights Act of 1965.*

J.L. Chestnut, Jr. *Black in Selma: The Uncommon Life of J.L. Chestnut Jr.*

John Lewis. *Walking with the Wind: A Memoir of the Movement.* 1998.

March (comic book series). John Lewis and Andrew Aydin, illustrated by Nate Powell. Top Shelf
    Production.

Black Lives Matter

Chatelaine, Marcia. "Teaching the #FergusonSyllabus." Dissent Magazine, November 28, 2014.

Killing Trayvons: An Anthology of American Violence. Kevin Alexander Gray, author. JoAnn Wypijewski,
    Jeffrey St. Clair, editors. Counterpunch, 2014.

Taylor, Keeanga. *From #BlackLivesMatter to Black Liberation.* Haymarket Books. 2016.

Freedom Riders Greyhound Bus Station

Across That Bridge: Life Lessons and a Vision for Change. John Lewis. Hatchette Books, 2012.

American Experience: Freedom Riders. PBS/Stanley Nelson. 2011.

Freedom Riders: 1961 and the Struggle for Racial Justice. Raymond Arsenault. Oxford University Press,
    2006.

*The Politics of Injustice: The Kennedys, the Freedom Rides, and the Electoral Consequences of a Moral
    Compromise.* David Niven. University of Tennessee Press, 2003.

Audubon Ballroom

Growing Up X. Ilyasah Shabazz. One World/Ballentine, 2009.

Malcolm X, the film. Spike Lee, Warner Brothers 1992.

Malcolm X: A Life of Reinvention. Manning Marable. Viking Press. 2011.

The Autobiography of Malcolm X. Alex Haley, Malcolm X. New York Grove Press, 1965.

X: A Novel. Ilyasah Shabazz, Kekla Magoon. Candlewick Press, 2015.

Lorraine Motel / Martin Luther King Jr.

As Good as Anybody. Richard Michelson. Knopf Books for young readers, 2008.

Black Prophetic Fire. Cornel West and Christa Buschendorf. Beacon Press 2014.

D'Army Bailey. *Mine Eyes Have Seen: Dr. Martin Luther King Jr.'s Final Journey.* 1993.

D'Army Bailey. *The Education of a Black Radical: A Southern Civil Rights Activist's Journey, 1959-1964.* LSU Press, 2009.

Medgar Evers

Local People: The Struggle for Civil Rights in Mississippi. John Dittmer. University of Illinois Press. 1995.

Medgar Evers: Mississippi Martyr. Michael Vinson Williams. University of Arkansas Press, 2011.

Remembering Medgar Evers: Writing the Long Civil Rights Movement. Minrose Gwin. University of Georgia Press, 2013.

The Autobiography of Medgar Evers: A Hero's Life and Legacy Revealed Through His Writings, Letters and Speeches. Myrlie Evers-Williams, Manning Marable. Basic Books, 2006.

Modjeska Simkins

A Perfect Equality: Conflicts and Achievements of Historic Black Columbia. Catherine Fleming Bruce, South Carolina ETV.

At the Dark End of the Street: Black Women, Rape and Resistance – A New History of the Civil Rights Movement from Rosa Parks to the Rise of Black Power. Danielle McGuire. 2010. Random House.

Bedingfield, S. *Beating Down the Fear: The Civil Sphere and Political Change in South Carolina, 1940-1962.* Doctoral dissertation, University of South Carolina, 2014.

Crespino, Joseph. *Strom Thurmond's America.* 2013. Strauss and Farrar, New York.

Crosby, Emily. *Civil Rights: History From the Ground Up. Local Struggles, A National Movement.* University of Georgia Press 2011.

Finney, Nikkey. H*ead Off and Split.* Northwestern University Press.

Gay, Katheryn, editor. *American Dissidents: A Handbook of Troublemakers, Subversives, and Prisoners of Conscience.* ABC-CLIO, LLC. California. 2012.

Glasrud, Pitre. *Southern Black Women in the Modern Civil Rights Movement.* Texas A&M University 2013.

Honey, Michael K. *Going Down Jericho Road: The Memphis Strike, Martin Luther King's Last Campaign.* WW Norton. NY. 2007.

Jerome, Kate Bohem. *Columbia and the State of South Carolina: Cool Stuff Every Kid Should Know.* Arcadia Publishing.2012.

Kennedy, Randall. *For Discrimination: Race, Affirmative Action and the Law.* Random House books 2013.

Making a Way Out of No Way – Modjeska Simkins: Portrait of the Human Rights Activist. Beryl Dakers, South Carolina ETV.

Modjeska-Organization of American Historians.
   http://www.oah.org/pubs/magazine/women/hanson.htm

Omer and Appleby. *The Oxford Handbook of Religion, Conflict and Peacebuilding.* Oxford University Press 2015.

Resolution passed in SC legislature on Modjeska's death. http://www.scstatehouse.net/sess109_1991-1992/bills/1452.htm

'The Story of *Briggs V. Elliott*, 1954', Southern Education Foundation.
   http://www.sefatl.org/pdf/The%20Story%20of%20Briggs%20v.%20Elliott.pdf

Books with References to Modjeska Simkins

Appiah, Kwame and Henry Louis Gates, eds. *Civil Rights: An A-Z Reference of the Movement that Changed America.* Running Press, 2005.

Bass, Jack and Jack Nelson. *The Orangeburg Massacre.* Mercer University Press, 1999.

Chappell, David L. *A Stone of Hope: Prophetic Religion and the Death of Jim Crow.* University of North Carolina Press, 2004.

Crawford, Vicky et. Al. *Women in the Civil Rights Movement: Trailblazers and Torchbearers, 1941-1965.* Indiana University Press, 1993.

Fosl, Catherine with Angela Davis. *Subversive Southerner: Anne Braden and the Struggle for Racial Justice in the Cold War South.* Palgrave MacMillan 2002.

Greil, Marcus. *The Shape of Things to Come: Prophecy in the American Voice.* Farrar, Straus and Giroux, 2006.

Grose, Philip G. *South Carolina at the Brink: Robert McNair and the Politics of Civil Rights.* University of South Carolina Press. 2006.

Horne, Gerald. *Black and Red: W.E. B. DuBois and the Afro-American Response to the Cold War: 1944-1963*. Suny Press, 1986.

Lau, Peter. *Democracy Rising: South Carolina and the Fight for Black Equality since 1865*. U. Kentucky Press, 2006.

Sales, William W. *From Civil Rights to Black Liberation: Malcolm X and the Organization of Afro-American Unity*. South End Press. 1994.

Sisters in the Struggle: African American Women in the Civil Rights and Black Power Movements. NYU press, 2001.

Smith, Jessie Carney, editor. *Notable Black American Women,* vol. I-III. Thomson Gale, 1991.

Ware, Susan, ed. *Notable American Women: A Biographical Dictionary*. Belknap Press of Harvard University Press, 2004.

Williams, Cecil J. *Freedom and Justice: Four Decades of the Civil Rights Struggle as Seen by a Black Photographer in the Deep South*. Mercer University Press, 1995.

Robben Island Prison / Nelson Mandela

Cohen, David Elliot and John D. Battersby. *Nelson Mandela: A Life in Photographs*. 2009.

Foster, Douglas. *After Mandela: The Struggle for Freedom in Post-Apartheid South Africa*. 2012.

Mandela, Nelson. *Long Walk to Freedom*. 1994.

Nelson, Kadir. *Nelson Mandela* (for Children)

Wilson, Frances. *Dinosaurs, Diamonds & Democracy: A Short, Short History of South Africa*. 2011.

Friendship Nine / McCrory Sit-ins

No Fear For Freedom: The Story of the Friendship 9. Kimberly P. Johnson. Frown-Free Publications, 2014.

Mother Emanuel AME Church

#Charlestonsyllabus, African American Intellectual History Society website, www.aaihs.org

Estes, Steve. *Charleston in Black and White: Race and Power in the South After the Civil Rights Movement.* UNC Press, 2015.

Frazier, Herb, et. Al. *We are Charleston: Tragedy and Triumph at Mother Emanuel.* Thomas Nelson, Publisher. June 2016 release.

Gillespie, J. David. *Race Murder, Christian Forgiveness, and Revolutionary Change in Charleston, South Carolina: A Seminal Moment in American History.* Edwin Mellen Press. Lewiston, NY: 2015.

Robertson, David M. *Denmark Vesey: The Buried Story of America's Largest Slave Rebellion and the Man who Led it.* Knopf Doubleday. 2009.

General Reading on Civil Rights, Human Rights and Social issues and Movements

Bhabha, Jacqueline. *Child Migration and Human Rights in a Global Age.* Princeton University Press, 2014.

Coates, Ta-Nehisi. *Between the World and Me.* Random House Publishing Group. 2015.

Encyclical Letter Laudato Si' of the Holy Father Francis on Care for our Common Home. Vatican Press, 2015.

Goldstone, Jack A., editor. *The Encyclopedia of Political Revolutions.* Congressional Quarterly, Inc. Washington DC, 1998.

Graham, Kevin M. *Beyond Redistribution: White Supremacy and Racial Justice.* Lexington Books, 2012.

Piketty, Thomas. *Capital in the Twenty-first Century.* Harvard University Press, 2014.

Spence, Lester. *Knocking the Hustle: Against the Neoliberal Turn in Black Politics.* Punctum Books, 2015.

Vidal, Gore. *Imperial America: Reflections on the United States of Amnesia.* Nation Books, 2005.

*

Additional Civil and Human Rights Sites

Selected Historical Marker, Statues and Monuments

ACCORD Freedom Trail and Civil Rights Museum, St. Augustine, FL

African American History Monument, Ed Dwight, Sculptor, South Carolina State House grounds, Sumter Street side, Columbia, SC

Black Panther's First Office, Martin Luther King Jr. Way, Oakland, CA

Black Power Speech/Stokely Carmichael, Broad St. and Avenue M., Greenwood, MS

Civil Rights Wayside signs, Main Street, Columbia, SC

Denmark Vesey statue, Hampton Park, Charleston, SC

Dred and Harriet Scott, Old Courthouse, Market St. and 4th St., Saint Louis, MO

Fannie Lou Hamer Memorial Garden, Byron St., Ruleville, MS

Freedom Riders, Albert P. Brewer Highway, Anniston, AL

Freedom Summer Murders/James Chaney, Andrew Goodman and Michael Schwerner, Route 19, Philadelphia, MS

Jackie Robinson, Journal Square Transportation Center, Jersey City, NJ

J. Waties Waring bronze statue, Richard Weaver, sculptor, J. Waties Waring Judicial Center, Meeting and Broad Streets, Charleston, SC

Kunte Kinte/Alex Haley Memorial, Maine and Compromise St., Annapolis, MD

Massacre at Wounded Knee, Pine Ridge Indian Reservation, SD

McCrory Civil Rights Sit-Ins/"Friendship Nine", Main Street, Rock Hill, SC

Montgomery's Slave Depots, Montgomery, AL

Rosewood, Route 24, Rosewood, FL

Septima P. Clark Parkway, intersection of Septima Clark Expressway (U.S. 17) and President Street, Charleston, SC.

Solomon Northrup "author ' 12 Years a Slave, Broadway Near Congress St., Saratoga Springs, NY

Student Nonviolent Coordinating Committee (SNCC), Shaw University, Raleigh, NC

The Anti-slavery community, Park and Meadow Sts., Florence, MA

The Bus Stop/Montgomery Bus Boycott/Rosa Parks, Dexter Avenue and Commerce St., Montgomery, AL

The Domestic Slave Trade, Riverfront, Montgomery, AL

The Forty Acres, Cesar Chavez United Worker Movement, Delano, CA

The Frank M. Johnson, Jr. Federal Building and United States Courthouse, Lee Street, Montgomery, AL

Thurgood Marshall, 'Equal Justice Under the Law', Lawyer's Mall, State House Square, Annapolis, MD

Thurgood Marshall House, Division Street, Baltimore, MD

Warehouses Used in The Slave Trade, Commerce Street, Montgomery, AL

Women's Rights National Park, Seneca, NY

National Register of Historic Places Sites

All-Star Bowling Lanes, Orangeburg, SC

Andrew Rankin Memorial Chapel, Frederick Douglass Memorial Hall, and Founders Library, Washington DC

Atlanta Center University Historic District, Atlanta, Georgia

Bethel AME Church, Reno, NV

Butler Chapel AME Zion Church, Tuskegee, Alabama

Calvary Baptist Church, Oklahoma City

Dexter Avenue Pastorium, Montgomery, Alabama

Dorchester Academy Boys' Dormitory, Midway, Georgia

Dunbar Apartments, New York, NY

Elizabeth Harden Gilmore House, Charleston, WV

First African Baptist Church, Tuscaloosa Alabama

First Baptist Church, Selma Alabama

F.W. Woolworth Building, Greensboro, NC

Howard Thurman House, Daytona Beach, Florida

Juanita Craft House, Dallas, TX

Lincolnville Historic District, St. Augustine, Florida

Malcolm X House Site, Omaha, NB

Mason Temple, Church of God in Christ, Memphis, TN

Moulin Rouge Hotel, Las Vegas, NV

Mount Zion Baptist Church, Albany, Georgia

New Kent School and George W. Watkins School, New Kent Co., Virginia

Sixteenth Street Baptist Church, Birmingham, Alabama

South Carolina College Historic District, Orangeburg, SC

Tougaloo College, Tougaloo, MS

US Post Office and Courthouse, Montgomery, Alabama

Waverly Historic District, Columbia, SC

West Park (Kelly Ingram Park) Birmingham, Alabama

Whitney Plantation, 5099 Hwy 18, Wallace LA 70049

National Historic Landmarks

Bizzell Library at the University of Oklahoma, Norman, OK

Daisy Bates House, Little Rock, AK

Dexter Avenue Baptist Church, Montgomery, Alabama

Edmund Pettus Bridge, Selma, AL

Fairchild-Stone Hall of Atlanta Center University Historic District, Atlanta, Georgia

Ida B. Wells-Barnett House, Chicago

John Philip Sousa Junior High School, Washington, DC

Lincoln Hall, Berea College, Berea, KY

Mary Church Terrell House, Washington DC

Oscar Stanton De Priest House, Chicago, IL

Paul Robeson Home, New York, NY

Robert Russa Moton High School, Farmville, Virginia

Shelley House, St. Louis, MO

W.E. B. Du Boise Homesite, Great Barrington, NY

Whitney M. Young Jr. Birthplace, Simpsonville, KY

William Monroe Trotter House, Dorchester, NY

National Park Service Sites

African Burial Ground National Monument, New York

Brown v. Board of Education National Historic Site, Topeka, KS

Lincoln Memorial, Washington, DC

Little Rock Central High School National Historic Site, Little Rock, AR

Martin Luther King, Jr. National Historic Site, Atlanta, Georgia

UNESCO World Heritage Site

Robben Island, South Africa

Selected International Sites of Conscience

Africa

Constitution Hill, South Africa

Kigali Memorial Center, Rwanda

Maison des Esclaves, Senegal

Workers Museum at Khanya College, South Africa

Zanzibar Former slave market, Tanzania

Asia

Jamalpur Gandhi Ashram, Bangladesh

Tuol Sleng Genocide Museum, Cambodia

Australia

Parramatta Female Factory Precinct Memory Project

Europe

Fondazione Scuola de Pace di Monte Sole, Italy

Historical Museum of the City of Krakow, Eagle Pharmacy, Pomorska Street, Poland

Jasenovac Memorial Site, Croatia

Le Bois du Cazier, Belgium

Le Route des Abolitions de L'esclavage Et Droits De L' Homme, France

Mauthausen Memorial, Austria

Museum of Tolerance, Serbia

Musee Memorial de l'Exile, Spain

Museo Storico Della Liberazione, Italy

Museum of Free Derry, Northern Ireland

Red Star Line Museum, Belgium

Schindler's Factory, Poland

Srebrenica – Potocari Memorial Center and Cemetery, Bosnia and Herzegovina

Terezin Memorial, Czech Republic

The Workhouse, United Kingdom

Latin America

Archivo Provincia de la Memoria, Cordoba, Argentina

Centro Cultural Por la Memoria la Trelew, Argentina

Comite de Derechos Hermanos, NIDO 20, Chile

Corporacion Parque Por la Paz Villa Grimalde, Chile

Memorial de Resistance de Sao Paulo, Brazil

Russia

Gulag Museum at Perm-36

United States of America

Andersonville National Historic Site

Bosque Redondo Site at Fort Sumner Historic Site

Eleanor Roosevelt Historic Site

Fort Apache/Theodore Roosevelt School

F.W. Woolworth Department Store/International Civil Rights Center and Museum, Greensboro, NC

Lower East Side Tenement Museum

Patrick Henry's Scotchtown

Manzanar National Historic Site

The Sixth Floor Museum

Tribute World Trade Center Visitor's Center

Women's Rights National Historic Park

Resource Organizations

African American Heritage Preservation Foundation (AAHPF)
www.aahpfdn.org
420 Seventh St., NW Suite 501
Washington DC 20004-2211

Asistencia Legal por los Derechos Humanos
www.asilegal.org.mx

Avery Research Center, College of Charleston
avery.cofc.edu
125 Bull St.
Charleston, SC 29424

Black Lives Matter
www.Blacklivesmatter.com

Environmental Health Science
Cassandra Williams Rush, CEO
213 Miles Road
Columbia, SC 29223

Equal Justice Initiative
www.eji.org
122 Commerce Street
Montgomery, AL 36104

Fannie Lou Hamer Institute @ COFO
Jackson State University
P.O. Box 17081
Jackson, Mississippi 39217

Five & Dine History in the Tasting
McCrory building, Friendship Nine sit-in site
135 E. Main St., #101
Rock Hill, SC 29730

FrameWorks Institute
1333 H St., NW Suite 700 West
Washington, DC 20005

Freedom Rides Museum
www.preserveala.org/greyhoundstation.aspx
210 S. Court St., Montgomery, AL 36104

Geronimos Environmental Consultants
Michael Geronimakis, President
7 Clusters Ct.
Columbia SC 29210

Harriet Tubman Underground Railroad National Monument National Park Service
www.nps.gov/hatu/index.htm
c/o Blackwater National Wildlife Refuge
2145 Key Wallace Drive
Cambridge, MD 21613

Historic Columbia Foundation
www.historiccolumbia.org
1601 Richland St.
Columbia, SC 29201

Historical Marker Database
www.HMdb.org
J.J. Prats, Publisher

Human Rights Center
www.law.berkeley.edu/hrc.htm
University of California, Berkeley
2850 Telegraph Ave., #500
Berkeley, CA 94705

International Coalition of Sites of Conscience
www.sitesofconscience.org
10 West 37th St., 6th Floor
New York, NY 10018 USC

King Center for Social Change
www.thekingcenter.org
449 Auburn Avenue, NE
Atlanta, GA 30312

Medgar Evers Home Museum
2332 Margaret Walker Alexander Drive
Jackson, MS 39213

Middle Passage Ceremonies and Port Markers Project, Inc.
P O Box 3071
Jacksonville, FL 32206

National Archives and Records Administration
www.archives.gov
8601 Adelphi Road
College Park, MD 20740-6001

National Civil Rights Museum/At the Lorraine Motel
Civilrightsmuseum.org
450 Mulberry St.
Memphis, TN 38103

National Park Service
www.nps.gov
US Department of the Interior
1849 C Street NW
Washington, DC 20240

National Trust for Historic Preservation
www.preservationnation.org
The Watergate Office Building
2600 Virginia Avenue, Suite 1000
Washington, DC 20037

National Voting Rights Museum and Institute
www.nvrmi.com
1012 Water Ave.
Selma, AL 36701

Penn Center
Penncenter.com
16 Penn Center Cir W
St. Helena Island, SC 29920

Robben Island Museum
www.robben-island.org.za
Private Bag Robben Island
Cape Town 7400

Robben Island Museum
Nelson Mandela Gateway
P. O. Box 51806
V&S Waterfront
Cape Town 8002

Rodgers Boykin
Artist, Fine Arts
1916 Kathleen Drive
Columbia, SC 29210
rodgersbboykin@gmail.com

Selma to Montgomery National Historic Trail
www.nps.gov/semo/index.htm
Lowndes Interpretive Center
7002 US Highway 80
P.O. Box 595
Hayneville, Alabama 36040

Selma to Montgomery National Historic Trail
Selma Interpretive Center
2 Broad Street
Selma, AL 36701

National Museum of African American History and Culture
Nmaahc.si.edu
Smithsonian Institute
Washington DC 20013

Southern Regional Council
www.southerncouncil.org
1201 West Peachtree St., NE Suite 2000
Atlanta, GA 30309

The Civil Rights Project/Proyecto Derechos Civiles
civilrightsproject.ucla.edu
8370 Math Sciences Box 951521
Los Angeles, CA 90095-1521

The Malcolm X and Dr. Betty Shabazz Memorial and Educational Center
Theshabazzcenter.net
3940 Broadway
New York City, NY 10032

Center for Civil Rights History and Research
sccivilrights@sc.edu
University of South Carolina
Columbia, South Carolina

Tnovsa, LLC
Visanska Starks House and Carriage House
P.O. Box 50055 tnovsacfb@gmail.com
Columbia, SC 29250

New York Public Library/Schomburg Center for Research in Black Culture
515 Malcolm X Boulevard   www.nypl.org/locations/schomburg
New York, New York 10037

UNESCO World Heritage Center
7 Place de Fontenoy
75352 Paris, France CEDEX 07
Whc.unesco.org

Hands Up United
224 N. Hwy 67, Suite 226
Florissant, MO 63031
www.handsupunited.org

About the author

Catherine Fleming Bruce is Principal at TNOVSA, focused on media, politics, preservation and global projects. The author's personal journey as a sustainer of civil and human rights legacy sites led to curiosity about others who fought for the survival of locations where critical events in the civil and human rights movement had taken place. The author's path: the home of South Carolina civil rights activist Mary Modjeska Monteith Simkins and the Visanska Starks House and Carriage House in Columbia, South Carolina.

She is an alumna of Agnes Scott College, with degrees in English/Creative Writing and Art. She is also a graduate of the University of South Carolina, receiving her Master of Arts in Mass Communication and Information Studies and took doctoral-level courses in philosophy, international relations, mass communication and information studies, and international law. Her global work has included presentations for the University of South Carolina's Walker Institute of International and Area Studies, at Les Instituts d'Etudes Politiques (IEP) in France, and serving as a United Nations World Summit for the Information Society observer. Other publications include 'The globalization-friendly public sphere: contrasting paths to moral legitimacy and accountability" in *Public Sphere Reconsidered: Theories and Practices* (2012).

She has held positions with several statewide institutions, including South Carolina Educational Television, Claflin University, the South Carolina Humanities Council, and currently, Palmetto Project. She remains active in social change efforts statewide. She is currently working on a book about her father, Louis Fleming, a South Carolina County Council Chairman and litigant in a voting rights case that went to a US Supreme Court panel. She has one son, Alaric Bruce.

Made in the USA
Middletown, DE
17 January 2018